HEROES

THE TITANS OF HISTORY

CHRISTOPHER R. MATTIX

Translated from *"Héroes: Titanes de la fe"*
Spanish Version by Mark Mattix
Originally published by Editorial Desafío 2017

Correction of style: Maureen Lytle, Suzanne Hurtado,
Jeremiah Mattix
Design and Layout: tribucreativos.com
Illustrations: Carlos Andrés Celis

Published and Distributed by Christopher Mattix
facebook.com/CRMattix
recursoscristianos.info

Category: Biography, Church History
ISBN: 978-958-52993-0-6

Printed in Colombia

CONTENT:

DEDICATION

Soli Deo gloria

PREFACE

We have been told that a hero is the warrior who rescues the princess and raises his blood-stained sword above the slain dragon, or that the man wearing a cape and a mask and accomplishing impossible feats is a superhero. In the end, we can end up idolizing myths and making heroes out of people for some special talent without considering their character. Should someone be considered a hero because of what he wears or what he has or because of some ability he has been given?

True heroes are those who deserve to be imitated because of their valor and the character they possess: Loving unconditionally, being the voice of the innocent and a defender of truth at any cost.

The true hero follows the steps of the One who, because of His love for us chose an animal's trough, a carpenter's hammer, and the cross of a criminal. Has there ever been a king who washed his followers' feet or who died loving his enemies? The most majestic, sublime, and transformative Being in history is Jesus, the carpenter of Nazareth, who soon will take His place as the King of kings. Napoleon Bonaparte, even though he was no Christian, concluded, "Alexander the Great, Caesar, Charlemagne, and I have founded empires. But what was the basis of our brilliant creations? Power. Jesus Christ founded His empire on love, and even now millions of men are willing to die for Him."

In the Bible we find great heroes, many who foreshadowed the essential virtues which are found perfectly represented in Jesus. For example, we could recall the story of Joseph, who was sold into slavery by his own family. He never lost his hope, he was faithful to God and overcame all obstacles until he became a great man of virtue and love. When he came to power, he had the opportunity to avenge himself of his cruel brothers, but instead he found his victory in forgiveness and went on to bless them and pay back good for evil.

King David protected Israel from many threats, none as great as the one posed by Goliath the giant, but it wasn't due to his slingshot that he gained the victory, but by his trust in God. Time and again David spared the life of those who wished to destroy him, even honoring the descendant of his enemy when he became king, giving him a place at his table.

When Daniel saw the danger to his life and the lives of all the wise men of Babylon, he didn't tremble in the presence of the imposing King Nebuchadnezzar, but rather he humbled himself before God and received crucial help. Then he ran to the king with the interpretation, saving not only his life but also those of the other wise men, his own rivals. He refused to seek honor for himself, choosing instead to save the lives of thousands and to give the glory to God.

The Apostle Paul found himself persecuted by Jews and Gentiles (non-Jews), suffering unfair insults and personal assaults, unjust imprisonment, and innumerable tortures, yet he never turned aside from his mission. His passion was to preach the truth of Jesus to a world inundated by materialism and idolatry. He died for this cause, yet not with the sorrow of a failed man, rather with the joy of a victor.

Against all odds, it is amazing to see how the Church which Jesus founded survived and even thrived in the face of persecution, but the story doesn't end with the book of *Acts*. The history of the Church goes on to tell innumerable stories of great men and women over the last two millennia: men and women of integrity, perseverance, and passionate love. In short, they are heroes of the highest level, worthy to be imitated, and admired for their love of the truth. They protected the truth of the Word of God, even though they had to suffer the persecution of perverse rulers, resist the corruptions and heresies of greedy men, bear the tortures of the Holy Inquisition, and so much more. The most surprising thing is that these heroes accomplished such feats without the use of weapons or political support, but by placing their faith in a living God, Who moves mountains and fights on behalf of those who love Him. God used these great men and women to defend the true Church, to stand for righteousness, and preserve the message of Jesus, the One who came to save the world from its sins through His sacrifice on the cross. Here we observe how the greatest transformative power in the world is a pure love, the love of God.

> **Against all odds, it is amazing to see how the Church which Jesus founded survived and even thrived in the face of persecution, but the story doesn't end with the book of Acts.**

I invite you to get to know better the story of eight of the most extraordinary men who laid foundations in the history of the Church and to see how they helped preserve the truth of the Word of God. We will see the implacable courage of Polycarp, the perseverance of Athanasius, the power of grace which transformed Augustine of Hippo, the love for Christ which moved Francis of Assisi, the unmovable faith of Martin Luther, the longsuffering patience of William Tyndale, the passion for souls which motivated George Whitefield, and the constant joy which sustained George Muller.

Here are only some of the heroes who have inspired and transformed so many lives. Even though they are dead, their amazing stories echo through the years to all who are ready to hear and to learn from them. Let me invite you to get to know them.

CHAPTER 1

POLYCARP OF SMYRNA

Imagine that you are traveling in the Middle East and suddenly you are captured by a group of radical Islamic terrorists. They put you in a filthy cell, tying your hands together and placing a dirty sack over your head. After being without food for days they haul you outside and violently make you kneel. You feel the infernal desert heat burning your skin and sunlight so strong that you feel like fainting. They rip off the sack which was tied on your head and gradually you are able to see that you are surrounded by a crowd of men dressed in black, all holding massive machine guns and long, curved swords which glitter in the sunshine. There is a camera in front of you and you are being filmed. Suddenly, you feel the edge of a sharp sword on the back of your neck.

"Is Jesus the Son of God?" a powerful man shouts down at you. He has his face covered with a black mask with Arabic writing on it.

What would you say? Would you be willing to give your life for your faith in Christ as your God and Savior?

Polycarp of Smyrna

69 - 156 A.D.

Unfortunately, such scenes are a routine occurrence in the Middle East in our times, and doubtless this situation will continue to worsen. Yet it is not a new dilemma. It is part of being a follower of Christ. What should a Christian do when they are is faced with torture or death on account of their faith?

Jesus declared, "And I tell you, everyone who acknowledges me before men, the Son of Man also will acknowledge before the angels of God, but the one who denies me before men will be denied before the angels of God" (Luke 12:8-9, *ESV*).

What would you say? Would you be willing to give your life for your faith in Christ as your God and Savior?

One of the great heroes of the faith in the history of the Church was Polycarp, a leader of the church in Smyrna, which is Izmir in modern day Turkey. He refused to deny Christ, demonstrating humility, yet also revealing inner strength as he showed his faith in the face of the ruling authorities of those days.

Polycarp was born in the year 69 A.D. and died as a martyr in 156 A.D. He was a disciple of the last of Jesus' disciples to die, the Apostle John. Can you imagine how much he may have learned from John, who was the Lord Jesus' closest friend? Under his mentorship, Polycarp came to be recognized among the churches at that time as a beloved leader, preacher, and writer. Even today, you can read several of his works. Most of them are expositions and commentaries of passages or books from the Bible.

Polycarp lived in an age which was exceedingly difficult for the Church, for they were suffering persecution by both the Jews and the Gentiles and, at times, by the Roman Empire itself. The Jews hated them because they thought the Christians were distorting Old Testament teachings since they could not accept that Jesus was their Messiah. The Gentiles hated them because they saw how the believers lived a different lifestyle and that thousands were leaving the Greco-Roman religion to join them. Instead of trying to understand them, they preferred to make up rumors in order to vilify them, spearheaded by leaders of the false religion who doubtless made a handsome living off the sale of idols and votive offerings. Some Roman emperors and governors of different cities also targeted the Christians, wanting to shame them publicly and in that way show their support for the official religion.

One of them was the Emperor Nero – a violent, ambitious, and power-crazed man. It is said that he assassinated his mother, decapitated his wife, and violently killed his pregnant concubine by kicking her to death, simply because he had heard rumors that they wished to usurp his authority. In his ambition, he also decided to burn down outlying neighborhoods of Rome in order to build more theaters, coliseums, and parks. And who did he decide to blame? The Christians, a small, hated and misunderstood minority.

Over the years the hatred and resentment against the believers was only intensified, especially when people saw how the Church of Christ kept on growing in a surprising way. The governor of the city of Smyrna decided to do something about it and he ordered the arrest of the most renowned Christian of the region, the elder Polycarp. This recognized leader of the Christians was arrested for refusing to offer a little bit of incense to the Roman Emperor, a common practice among the pagans. Occasionally the government in Rome would order its people to line-up to throw a little bit of incense upon the altar in honor of the emperor. Once they fulfilled this small duty, they received a letter called the *libellus* which served as personal identification, which proved that they were loyal citizens. Christians refused to offer this incense to the emperor because they saw this, not as a political act, but as a religious one. God had said: "You shall worship no other god" (*Exodus 34:14a*).

Would you risk execution simply because you didn't throw a tiny bit of incense on an altar? That was the question that believers had to answer in that time of terrible persecution.

Polycarp became a great example of valor and faithfulness to the Lord when he refused to offer incense to the emperor. He was 86 years old when the governor's soldiers came to his home to arrest him for this "crime." He went out and greeted them cheerfully, inviting them into his house for a bite to eat. History relates how the soldiers were surprised and accepted Polycarp's offer, sitting down to eat with the old man before arresting him.

When it came time to arrest him, the soldiers felt sorry for him being so elderly and in poor health. They told him they would grant him liberty if he would just say that Caesar is god. Polycarp answered them firmly, "For 86 years I have served God and He has never done me harm. How could I now blaspheme against my King and Savior?" The soldiers were stunned to see the old man's conviction, yet they had to take him in.

The governor of Smyrna then organized a grand event to publicize the death of the famous Christian, Polycarp. The central coliseum was packed with people eager to see blood flow, with the lions pulling anxiously against the heavy chains that held them back. Polycarp, chained up and draped with rags like a criminal, was presented before the governor and the expectant multitude in the grandstands, who booed him feverishly.

"You must only vow loyalty to Caesar," the governor declared, giving the old man a final opportunity.

"I am a Christian," Polycarp replied, "if you wish to understand what this means, give me one day and I will explain it to you."

"Persuade the populace," said the governor, pointing to the blood-thirsty masses.

"I desire to explain it to you, but not to them," responded Polycarp, trying to secure an opportunity to share his faith in a setting where he would have a fair hearing.

"Then … I will throw you to the lions!" shouted the governor, and all the people echoed his words.

"Bring on your lions!" Polycarp bellowed back, standing firm upon the arena of the enormous coliseum.

"Since you laugh at the lions, I'll order you to be burnt alive," responded the governor, with a sinister smile.

"You wish me to fear a fire which will burn for merely one hour," the old saint responded firmly, "yet you forget about the fire of hell which can never be extinguished!"

Then the governor hollered to the crowd of people, "Polycarp says he is a Christian."

The people responded by making their will known: "This is the teacher of all Asia, the father of the Christians, the one who destroys our gods!" In their wrath, they thus confirmed his death sentence.

In this way, Polycarp, praying aloud for the Lord to accept his life as a sacrifice, was burnt alive at the stake.

What I just told you is true. It really happened.

And you, would you be ready to declare your love for God and give your life for Him? Jesus clearly states what He expects of His true disciples:

"If anyone would come after me, let him deny himself and take up his cross and follow me. For whoever would save his life will lose it, but whoever loses his life for my sake and the gospel's will save it. For what does it profit a man to gain the whole world and forfeit his soul? For what can a man give in return for his soul? For whoever is ashamed of me and of my words in this adulterous and sinful generation, of him will the Son of Man also be ashamed when he comes in the glory of his Father with the holy angels." (Mark 8:34-38)

THE PEOPLE'S PERSECUTION, 33 TO 250 A.D.

During this time, the movement of Jesus' followers blossomed to international recognition. Jesus' radical teachings attracted countless people of every race, nation, and creed. The leaders of other religions were filled with jealousy and circulated malicious rumors about the Christians who started coming under persecution, rejection, and martyrdom in many parts of the Roman Empire. Christians had to hide in caves, in underground cemeteries (known as catacombs), or in forests. Since the public in general didn't know the truth of what the Christians taught, their enemies invented rumors so that the people would be predisposed to hate them.

Here are 5 of the most common rumors from that time:

1. "Political rebels" – even though they were respectful of the government and paid their taxes, they did not worship Caesar and that was viewed as treason.

2. "Haters of mankind" – that's what the Roman historian Tacitus called them because they were deemed separatists for not taking part in the abominable immoralities of the Greco-Roman culture.

3. "Atheists" – they didn't have statues or ostentatious temples. They only worshiped an invisible God.

4. "Cannibals" – a mistaken interpretation of the Lord's Supper. What did they think when they heard, "this is my body" and "this is my blood"?

5. "Sexually immoral" – a misunderstanding of the use of "brother" and "sister" in the Church. This brought down accusations of incest, with their detractors trying to pull them down to their own level of sexual depravation.

THE OFFICIAL PERSECUTION, 250 TO 311 A.D.

When Decius became emperor, once again the Roman Empire was under attack from the East. The Christian movement was now bigger than ever, for the persecutions had only intensified their love for Christ. The emperor put forth the popular idea that the Roman Empire was going through hard times because they were no longer faithful to their Greco-Roman gods. The "Edict of 250" was passed, which declared that everyone must offer incense to Caesar or face the pain of death. Most Christians opposed this rule and innumerable believers were tortured, jailed, sent to the lions, crucified, etc. Despite it all, the church still grew.

Years later, Emperor Diocletian – and after that, Emperor Galerius – mounted the worst persecution of the Church in all of history, known as the "Great

> *Despite it all, the church still grew.*

Persecution" (300 to 311 A.D.). Christianity was declared illegal. Churches and Bibles were burned, and persecution got so bad that it seemed it would be impossible for Christianity to survive. Even so, though it's hard to believe, the Church continued to thrive. Tertullian, a Christian historian, tells us about the perseverance and faith of these believers by stating: "The blood of the martyrs is the seed of the Church." On his deathbed Emperor Galerius recognized that he had been conquered, not by armies, but by the promise of Christ to his beloved Church (*Matthew 16:18*). In 311 A.D. he signed the "Edict of Tolerance," putting an end to the widespread persecution.

CHAPTER 2

ATHANASIUS OF ALEXANDRIA

Dr. Martin Luther King, Jr. was a black Christian who fought for the rights of his people in the United States in the 1960's. He declared, "A man who does not have something for which he is willing to die is not fit to live." Dr. King was assassinated by an enemy of the blacks, while in the prime of life. He left the legacy of having defended human equality the way God had declared it to be in His Word.

And you, do you have something for which you would be willing to die?

Athanasius of Alexandria (296-373 A.D.) is one of the heroes of the faith because he was willing to give his honor and even his life to defend the primary, non-negotiable doctrines of the Word of God. To understand this person and the dangers he faced, we first need to understand the context in which he lived.

And you, do you have something for which you would be willing to die?

Athanasius of Alexandria

296-373 A.D.

The Church suffered greatly in the first three centuries, threatened by both Jews and Gentiles who hated and persecuted them. Led by Emperor Decius, the government itself began to cruelly persecute the Church, starting in 250 A.D. with the stated intention of eradicating Christianity from the face of the earth. They failed. During the next sixty years this official persecution intensified. In 303, perhaps the most fearsome of all the emperors appeared, Diocletian. He filled the whole empire with soldiers and spies that sought out the Christians everywhere, attempting to fulfill the Decius' edict which never had fulfilled its goal. Thousands upon thousands of Christians were tortured, jailed, massacred, given to the lions, crucified or cut in pieces by gladiators. The public loved such spectacles, yet the believers' faithfulness and valor became something they could not explain.

Then a general showed up who wanted the empire for himself and in 313 A.D. he achieved it, assuming the title of Emperor Constantine. Immediately, this new emperor surprised the whole empire by publishing the "Edict of Milan" that very same year. This new order declared that Christianity was no longer illegal; from now on it was to be the favored religion of the empire! It was a drastic turnaround and transformed human history forever. Men and women who before had once had to hide in secret places and catacombs now had royal support for the pursuit of their religion.

Why such a radical change of policy? Constantine declared that God Himself had met him in a vision, and in that vision, he had been told how to win the throne of the empire. That said, Constantine never changed his way of life and only was baptized on the day of his death, showing that he probably never was a real Christian. Then, how do we explain this paradigm shift?

If there is something that needs to be understood about world history it is that the great decisions are always taken for one of the three following reasons: power, money or love. In this case, it was the first, being the most common and dangerous of all three reasons. Astute readers will recognize that the simplest name for this trend is what we call politics. Constantine saw that Christianity had become the most popular religion in the empire and that the more it was persecuted, the more it grew. As the adage goes, "If you can't beat them, join them." Constantine saw how advantageous it would be for him to have Christianity as the state religion and so he sought in this way to please the people and pacify the masses.

> *If there is something that needs to be understood about world history it is that the great decisions are always taken for one of the three following reasons: power, money or love.*

Christians thanked God for His goodness and grace because what had happened to them was beyond their imagination. One day they were persecuted by Roman soldiers and the next day they were given protection by the emperor himself. But, when the persecution died down, another terrible danger appeared – false teachers. Many of the former pagan priests of the Greco-Roman religions with their plethora of gods now desired to "convert" and become Christians. As I like to tell my students, "Everyone and his dog wanted to become Christians now." Those priests who switched their allegiance to the Christian Church knew little about the Bible or Christ because for them religion was just a hobby, a way to manipulate the masses and an easy way to make a living.

For this reason, Christian historians call this epoch the "Age of Heresies," because Christianity was inundated by a myriad of new doctrines, ideas, and traditions borrowed from other religions. Some declared that there was only a single God and denied the Trinity. Others said that Jesus was a phantom that never had human flesh and thus never actually died. Others announced that they would only accept the part of the Bible written to Gentiles, in this manner cutting out of their Bible everything that wasn't written by Paul and Luke. Yet others declared that there were three distinct gods, rejecting the unity of God as expressed in the doctrine of the Trinity.

The most popular heresy, and thus the most dangerous of all, was Arianism. Arianism was the greatest danger hounding the Church in this era, being propounded by a charismatic preacher from North Africa by the name of Arius. He taught a false doctrine about Jesus, saying that this Jesus was the first of God's creations, that he was literally the son of God in the sense of having a beginning. Then, later, Jesus created the universe and eventually came into the world as the Scriptures declared. It was a slight variation; Arius did say that Jesus was a god, but not *the* Sovereign God. With this teaching he rejected the perfect deity of Christ and even disparaged the Trinity. This heresy became so popular and there was such an ignorance of the truth, that it was estimated that at the height of its popularity nine out of every ten church leaders supported it!

The Emperor Constantine saw it as problematic to have a divided Church, so he decided to call a council to quiet the ten percent who didn't let the people have peace. We can see that Constantine didn't care about truth; he simply wanted to pacify the public, arguing that religion first and foremost ought to bring peace, not discussions and fights. Yet can there be lasting peace without the truth?

In 325 A.D. the Council of Nicaea came together right in the palace of the emperor in the city of Nicaea, located in modern Turkey. Three hundred leaders were present, among them a young deacon named Athanasius who came from the city of Alexandria in Egypt. This man was accompanying the senior elder of the church, Alexander. Alexander defended orthodoxy (or "the truths of the Bible") and his arguments were so strong that it changed the other leaders' way of thinking, turning them against Arius. It was finally decided that Arianism was heresy and ought to be repudiated and to seal the conviction they wrote the famous "Nicene Creed." This document was centered on the declaration that the Lord Jesus Christ is fully God and man:

> *[We believe] in one Lord, Jesus Christ, the Son of God, begotten from the Father, only-begotten, that is, from the substance of the Father, God from God, light from light, true God from true God, begotten not made, of one substance with the Father...*

With only two refusing to sign the document, everyone said farewell; they were pleased and in great unity. So where does Athanasius come in? At that time, he was only a young deacon who was present at the event. The sad reality is that the leaders who composed and signed that document quickly abandoned the truth that they had declared there, taking once again Arius' side. Perhaps Arius was a tremendous preacher and writer, managing to sway the masses once again, even convincing their leaders. Perhaps the leaders didn't feel the urgency of defending the primary truths of the Bible, since many saw Christianity as a job instead of as the center of their life. It is probable that these two factors were an influence, yet perhaps nothing was as strong as the force of politics. Here we begin to see the terrible consequences of Christ's Church becoming yoked with the Roman Empire. Later, emperors, wanting to quiet the masses, took one side or the other of the debate between Arianism and orthodoxy, influenced not by the Bible, but by popular vote.

It was then that Athanasius, having since become an elder and leader of the church in Alexandria, began to raise his voice and his pen to defend the truth. During the greater part of his life he was part of that ten percent which repudiated Arianism as a diabolical teaching and grave threat to the Church. In his church he preached against Arianism using the Word of God as his basis, and always looking for new arguments to silence the lie of Arianism. Not many listened to him and many times he felt alone and abandoned. Even so, he resolved that he would never abandon God and His truth; even if everyone else denied it, he would stand firm.

Athanasius was an elder and leader of his church for forty-six years, but due to the political turbulence of the time he had to spend seventeen of those years living in the desert, exiled on five occasions having been deemed a disturber of the peace and a

I wonder if I would have kept my faith in such circumstances, living in caves amid the unbearable heat of the desert.

political traitor. Many tried to silence him, and others even attempted to kill him. I wonder if I would have kept my faith in such circumstances, living in caves amid the unbearable heat of the desert. I wonder if I would have the motivation and the courage to keep on like that without being able to speak with anyone else or preach the truth and without being able to use my gifts to edify others. Athanasius' suffering and loneliness were so great that he was known by the nickname *Athanasius Contra Mundum* (Athanasius against the World), in Latin.

This man never gave up: when they didn't let him preach or even walk the streets of Alexandria, being forced to live as a hermit, he saw a new opportunity. Some brothers from his church brought him his books, writing tools and papers so he could spend his days in deep study of the Word of God. He wrote a great quantity of books there, filling them with Biblical arguments against Arianism and proving that Christ had to be completely God and man in order to be our Savior. He argued that, if Christ were not God, then he wasn't perfect and only a perfect sacrifice could take away man's sin. He also argued that, if Christ were not man, then he couldn't have died on the cross in our place to pay for our sins. He concluded that Christ had to be completely God and completely man in one person, the exact definition of the Incarnation, a primary, non-negotiable doctrine of the Word of God.

In 373 A.D. Athanasius died, having made great efforts, yet without seeing many results. I wonder if he died with sadness and a heart full of prayers for the Church that he loved so much, which was falling apart before his eyes. He had no idea of the tremendous change which would come in just a few years. Theologians and historians have well asked, "If it hadn't been for Athanasius would we all be Arians today?"

It was in 381 A.D. that the second great council of the century was convened, this time by Emperor Theodosius I. Hundreds of church leaders got together to debate this subject once again, and again the vast majority were Arians. Those who argued for orthodoxy used the Bible as their center, with the tremendous and powerful support of Athanasius' books which had been published and spread all over the world. As they explained the arguments of Athanasius, now dead and buried, it is said that all were confounded by the logical and Biblical proofs of the late theologian. They concurred that the Nicene Creed ought to be defended in its totality and even took steps to bolster the teaching further. If anyone wouldn't accept the doctrine of Jesus' Incarnation as One who is fully God and fully man, they would be under the dire warning: "These the Universal and Apostolic Church anathematizes."

The faithfulness and courage of Athanasius is something which is very exemplary, seeing how he suffered so much to defend the name of Christ. He was willing to go against popular vote and leave behind his comfort to live as a hermit in the infernal heat of the desert. He did all this and more in order to defend the immovable conviction which he had in his God and Savior, the Lord Jesus Christ.

ARIANISM AND THE JEHOVAH'S WITNESSES

One would think that Arianism would remain buried after the efforts of Athanasius and the decision of the Church in the Council of Nicaea and Constantinople. Yet in 1872, more than one thousand years later, the ancient and dangerous heresy broke out anew in the form of the Jehovah's Witnesses. Surrounded by many false doctrines, greed, and methods of manipulation, this cult is based on the affirmation that Christ was just a man who became God by means of good works, leaving us an example of how to get to heaven by our own efforts. Just like the Arians, they are heretics because they deny the deity of Christ as well as the doctrine of the Trinity. Besides this, they teach salvation by works. Without doubt it is one of the most dangerous pseudo-Christian sects nowadays.

> *Without doubt it is one of the most dangerous pseudo-Christian sects nowadays.*

Thanks to Athanasius' exposition and the clarity of the Bible on these subjects, the modern Church had sufficient resources to absolutely uproot such lies. To counter this, the Jehovah's Witnesses committed another abominable heresy when they produced an aberrant translation of the Bible in 1961 to try to defend their claims.

CHAPTER 3

AUGUSTINE OF HIPPO

B y the fourth and fifth centuries Christianity became the official religion in what was left of the Roman Empire, yet few were those who truly embraced a relationship with God, preferring instead materialism and a wasted life. Others openly hated Christianity and one of them was Augustine, a famous orator and philosopher of the fourth century.

Augustine of Hippo (354-430 A.D.), who became one of the most influential Christians in history, was a real-life example of the Prodigal Son. Even though Augustine spent 32 years repudiating and walking away from the living God, God never ceased to pursue His lost son. After finding himself frustrated in his search of happiness and peace in the world, he found them in God. He later wrote, "You have made us for yourself, O Lord, and our hearts are restless until it finds its rest in you."

After surrendering his life to Christ, Augustine wrote his autobiography called *Confessions*, which has come to be one of

Augustine of Hippo
354-430 A.D.

the most important and most read in world history. In relating his story, in the form of a prayer of meditation and repentance to the Lord, he tells about his early rebellious years, his abhorrence of the Bible, and how he finally came to the light and found Christ.

Augustine was born in the small town of Tagaste in what is today known as the country of Algeria, being raised by working-class parents. His father was a drunkard, but his mother, Monica, was a pious woman, dedicated to the Lord. From an early age Augustine proved to be a prodigy and his genius was recognized by a rich citizen who offered to finance his studies. His parents decided to send him to Carthage, which was at that time the most important city in North Africa. Augustine later reflected on the fact that his parents were more concerned with his intellectual prowess than his spiritual health, a care which every father ought to take for his children since before God that is his responsibility.

In Carthage, free now from paternal care, the young Augustine began to misuse his time, getting together with friends who led him astray, leaving behind his mother's teachings. He came to hate the Bible, calling it "an outdated book" for "ignorant grandmothers." Augustine's intellect became evident in Carthage and soon excellent opportunities opened for him – he began to teach and to make good money at an early age.

His mother, who never stopped praying for him, came to see him in Carthage when her husband died. She was disconsolate when she saw how he had begun to waste his life; he hated God and His Word, he lived a life increasingly full of drunken parties, lewd women, and he had become quite an arrogant person. He had also acquired a concubine, something common in those times, and she served him as a slave and a lover. Even so, with all of this, his mother placed her faith in God's transforming power.

> But You, O Lord, made your hand felt from on high and delivered my soul from that black smoke because my mother, your faithful servant, wept for me more than other mothers weep at their son's funerals. She wept because of my spiritual deadness in that faith which you had given her, and you heard her cry. You heard when she sprinkled the earth with her tears before your eyes; she prayed for me everywhere and you heard her plea.

Augustine spent many more years wallowing in the filth of sin before his mother would see any answer to her prayers. His mother's company proved a frustration and so he decided to escape from Carthage secretly and go to the most important country of those times – Italy:

> For what reason did I want to leave Carthage and go to Rome, you already knew, but you didn't reveal it to me nor to my mother and she suffered terribly when I left secretly when she followed me to the edge of the sea. I deceived her, when she was holding on so tightly to me, trying to either keep me with her or accompany me. I pretended that I could not abandon a friend who was going to travel while the wind was favorable for sailing. In such a way I lied to that most extraordinary mother and I slipped away.

In Rome, Augustine enjoyed even more fame and greater opportunity. As in Carthage, Augustine pursued all kinds of philosophy and religion. His heart wished to find the truth and was willing to seek in any corner for such a truth, but never in Christ. In Carthage he had grown frustrated with the simplistic religion of the Manicheans and in Rome he soon began to repudiate the ancient, hollow philosophies of the Greeks. He also began to suffer a measure of poverty in the capital, since students there had grown accustomed to cheat their masters and tutors out of their due payment.

Like a dog following the smell of food, Augustine followed the road to glory and human riches, and the road led him now to Milan. By then his mother had found her way to Rome and so they went together to Milan. Only years later

> **His heart wished to find the truth and was willing to seek in any corner for such a truth, but never in Christ.**

did Augustine recognize the virtues of such a faithful mother. However, there was a local preacher who recognized them in his mother right away, his name being Ambrose of Milan.

> *Ambrose himself loved her for her religious conduct, for her fervor in good deeds and her faithful attendance to the church; he went so far as breaking out in her praises whenever he met me and he congratulated me for the blessing of having such a mother. This was because he did not know what a dreadful son my mother had: a skeptic who doubted everything and didn't believe it was even possible to find the way of truth.*

Augustine found in Milan what he was looking for – fame and riches. The Roman Senate resided there, and the doors opened for him to work for them and perhaps, in time, become one of that elite group. Soon he was recognized as one of the best orators and became famed for using his talents as a lawyer for despicable, yet wealthy criminals by securing their freedom. He thought he was living his dream, for he had become obsessed with reaching the pinnacle, yet once achieved, he was surprised at the fleeting vanity of it all.

One day, Augustine was hired to give a speech to the masses, and all the people crowded around him to hear his eloquence. Suddenly, the famous speaker saw a drunk beggar behind the crowd, walking happily among the garbage, looking for something to eat. Augustine could not explain why, but he felt tremendous envy of that beggar, and suddenly realized that that man enjoyed more happiness and peace than he did. Such is the futility and spiritual poverty of this world!

It was during this time that Augustine committed what at the time seemed like the worst mistake in his political career. Since his mother was a regular attender at a church in Milan where the eloquent Ambrose preached, she invited him time and again to go, until he finally accepted. He went with the excuse of studying the preacher, to find out why he was so famous and at the same time to use it to mock the Bible even more.

Augustine's visits became more and more frequent and in his heart a fire began to burn to know more about the Word of God. He had categorized the Bible as a myth, a story for children, but Ambrose's exposition of the Bible made him see that it was deeper and richer in meaning than the sea itself. In secret, Augustine began to study and to meditate on the Scriptures, and because of his pride he didn't dare tell his mother.

When he was 32, amid a terrible internal struggle, he decided to put his life entirely at God's disposal. He took a while in coming to this decision because he knew what many today do not realize – that Christ does not just call us simply to be saved, but to surrender ourselves to Him as our Owner and Master. Augustine struggled greatly with greed and love of power, but especially with lust, for he had decided to remain single if he converted to Christ.

During his mental anguish, Augustine felt God calling him to read in the scroll of Scripture which he had in his house. He opened it and read the following:

Let us walk properly as in the daytime, not in orgies and drunkenness, not in sexual immorality and sensuality, not in quarreling and jealousy. But put on the Lord Jesus Christ, and make no provision for the flesh, to gratify its desires. (Romans 13:13-14)

In these verses he found the strength to begin to leave his sinful lifestyle behind – the power of the Lord Jesus Christ. He also saw the importance of having mental strength to separate himself from the things which could make him stumble. Besides, Augustine now knew the power of the Holy Spirit, and reading these words he knew that he would not be alone in the ceaseless battle against sin and the devil.

He immediately went and told the glad news to his mother and to Ambrose, giving all the glory to God. Soon a public baptism was prepared so that everyone would know that Augustine was now part of the family of God. Since Augustine was a man of renown, many were left speechless at seeing him so repentant and humbled. This famous orator, a well-known enemy of Christianity, one who had bragged about his lewd lifestyle, his lust and his greed – here submerged under the waters of baptism!

Augustine wished to return to North Africa, wisely leaving behind the fame and the temptations that would surely bombard him in Italy. He hid away in the small town of Hippo and there began to study the Scriptures ardently, to preach with great impact and to write what became hundreds of books. Augustine is known today as perhaps the greatest theologian of all time, after only the Apostle Paul, and the great quantity of books which he wrote is nearly incomparable; among them his best-known work, *Confessions*.

He and his mother enjoyed a marvelous friendship and companionship until the end:

> *Being left alone, just the two of us, we began to talk, and the conversation was so sweet, because we forgot all the past and our discourse had to do with the consideration of things yet to come. We were pursuing that same truth, that you are and were present, that such was to be that eternal life which the saints are to enjoy, which consists of a happiness which eye has not seen nor ear heard nor is man able to imagine it.*

That day his mother entered heaven; she that he had so repudiated, yet now loved with all his being.

Augustine is a living example of the transforming power of God, of His infinite and unmerited grace. The great theologian has since been deemed "Dr. Grace," for he never stopped talking about the enormous love of God towards him and all people. He often stated that if God could change a wretch like him, who couldn't He use? This quote from Augustine underlines this point and gives the perfect conclusion to his surprising transformation: "The Church is not a cathedral for saints but a hospital for sinners."

WHERE DID SAINTS COME FROM IN THE ROMAN CATHOLIC CHURCH?

In order to defend their false doctrines, the Catholic Church depends a lot on lies which have been propagated about Augustine of Hippo. They say that the worship of virgins comes from the way Augustine treated his mother, Monica. The Catholic Church considers them both to be saints, with Augustine the more important of the two. Yet, did Augustine at any time teach the worship of the saints? Absolutely not! The church's practice of naming saints is something that came up hundreds of years later by priests which were evermore ignorant of the faith, even as the Catholic Church began to move away from its biblical basis and to become a heretical movement.

The teaching of the Roman Catholic Church is that, when one prays to the saints, they can share a little of their grace as they intercede for us in God's presence, and that this grace is accumulated during a lifetime to be able to get less time of suffering in the supposed purgatory. All too soon the Lord Jesus is reduced to a statue, an example of a martyr, and little more than a gruesome picture on a wall for people who are pursuing salvation by their own merits. The Catholic Church tries to rewrite history and tell us that Augustine taught such things. The life and the writings of Augustine show time and again that salvation is an undeserved and unconditional gift given by the only Savior and Intercessor, Jesus Christ.

If Augustine were alive today what would he say about the worship of idols? Would he teach salvation by works? Definitively not! Augustine, who left fame behind and intensely loved divine grace, would surely not identify with the Roman Catholic Church if he were alive today.

CHAPTER 4

FRANCIS OF ASSISI

If the Christian Church ever had a Golden Age, it was perhaps in the time of Augustine when great theologians arose and debated difficult doctrinal subjects, and the Gospel was clearly expounded throughout the whole known world.

In contrast, the following years leading up to the Reformation in 1517 A.D. were perhaps the darkest. Between the times of Augustine of Hippo and Francis of Assisi the Roman Empire fell, the "Dark Ages" occurred, a corrupt church hierarchy emerged, and the Gospel was nearly lost. The history of those events is long, confusing, and, above all, distressing. After the death of Francis, things would only get worse over the following 300 years before the rise of Martin Luther.

In Augustine's lifetime the Roman Empire had already begun to disintegrate. In 410, Rome was almost conquered by the Visigoths, a rebel confederation of warriors from the North, known in that time as "barbarians" because they were not civilized nor well-mannered. In 455, the Visigoths attacked once again, this time headed by the famed barbarous King Attila the Hun. Pope Leon the Great made a peace treaty

Francis of Assisi

1182–1226 A.D.

with Attila because the Roman Emperor had fled the city in a panic. Later, Leon tried to take the reins of government since there was no king and he declared himself the religious and political leader. It might be correct to say that he was the first one to believe himself to be a Pope as the single head of Christendom, although the populace repudiated his pretentions and he never managed to acquire the power that he coveted.

In 476, the Visigoths arrived for the third and last time, over-running Rome and sinking the whole empire into chaos, violence and anarchy. Because of this, the following 300 years are known as the "Dark Ages." In order to maintain their purity, a great number of Christians decided to go and live on the outskirts of the cities and towns, building small forts which would protect them from the constant wars between cities. These places were open to the people and functioned as churches, schools, and hospitals. The members who lived there gave themselves to communal work, to the careful study of the Word of God, to copying the Bible by hand, letter-by-letter, and to teaching the masses who came eagerly to them.

Eventually these places started limiting access to outsiders, with exaggerated rules imposed upon their members, including the prohibition of marriage and submission to their earthly leader as though he were divine. These places eventually came to be called monasteries, with their members known as monks and nuns, and their leaders going by the title of father. It's amazing how good beginnings turned into something evil and enslaving!

Later, an even greater danger arose, an enemy which seemed invincible – Islam. The Islamic Empire, founded by Mohammed in 630 in the deserts of Arabia, expanded at an enormous rate and in only 100 years it came to dominate all the Middle East and North Africa, also taking a good part of modern Turkey and Spain. In those days, there arose popes to replace the Roman Emperors in a political sense. The pope of that time was afraid of losing Europe and so he made an alliance with the powerful barbarian king of France, Charles "the Hammer" Martel, who surprised the world by defeating an enormous Muslim army in the "Battle of Tours" in the south of France in 732. Thanks to this victory, the pope declared this pagan army to be "Saviors of Europe" and sanctioned the rule of these Frankish kings over all of Europe. Soon afterwards, a later pope would rescind this authority based on a falsified document known as the "Donation of Constantine" which declared that God Himself had placed the pope as the supreme leader.

The grandson of Martel, the famous Charlemagne, is credited with bringing Europe out of the Dark Ages. He built schools and libraries, fomented the growth of arts and culture and, above all, the study of the Bible. His reign spawned the "Carolingian Renaissance," named in honor of Charlemagne, and it is recognized as the beginning of the Middle Ages which was between 800 and 1500 A.D., approximately.

It is in this era that we find our next hero, Francis (1182-1226), born in Assisi just north of Rome, in one of the most turbulent and corrupt times in the history of the Church. Francis lived in a world where they talked a lot about Christ, but few knew who He truly was or what it meant to be His disciple. That is why Francis is an enigma, a living contrast between what it means to serve Christ while the rest only play at religion.

The supreme leader during this time was Pope Innocent III. Although some argue that he himself was a God-fearing man, his cardinals loved heresy, war, and unjust gain. In the year 1215, they held the IV Lateran Council, an event which would forever con-

That is why Francis is an enigma, a living contrast between what it means to serve Christ while the rest only play at religion.

firm the Roman Catholic Church as heretical and completely contrary to the Word of God. In this council they declared the following: The Crusades would be used against the Muslims; the Holy Inquisition would be used against heretics and the Seven Sacraments would be recognized as the only means of Salvation.

The Crusades resulted in taking soldiers from across Europe and marching against the Islamic Empire, with the intention of taking back the Holy Land. Of the four great Crusades, only one managed to win back Jerusalem temporarily; they won the battle only to lose the war. Francis, who lived in these times and was forced to march in one such crusade, saw the terrible hypocrisy of doing such a thing in the name of Christ. Is this loving our enemies to take a sword and plunge it in their chests? In a poem he declared Christ's command to his followers:

Lord, make me an instrument of your peace,

Where there is hatred, help me to bring love;

Where there is strife, to bring forgiveness;

Where there are doubts, to bring faith;

Where there is despair, to bring hope;

Where there is darkness, to bring light;

Where there is sadness, to bring joy.

After failure to reconquer the Middle East, the blood-thirsty lust of the crusades was turned on the enemies of the Pope in Europe. The Holy Inquisition was created for enriching the Roman Catholic Church. It violated the basic laws which God had established for the protection of every human being. Thousands and thousands were arrested without clear evidence; they were rarely advised of their supposed crimes, they had no legal defense, and the inquisitor acted as their judge, torturer and executioner. All that belonged to them and to any family members was immediately confiscated by the Roman Catholic Church, and that is the reason the richest people were pursued most ferociously. Even though they might not be imprisoned or burned at the stake in the dreaded *auto de fé*, the public event where supposed "heretics" were burned alive, their goods were never returned to them.

Francis repudiated such acts and outspokenly preached against such abuses, striving to exemplify a different way with his life. He viewed the growing hypocrisy, how the priests and the cardinals slept in luxury and comfort surrounded by money and women while the people died of hunger and suffered the strangling fear of the seemingly omnipresent Inquisition. Seeing such extremes, Francis, who was part of the aristocracy, chose to identify himself with the people, dressing like them and giving away his riches to the poor. Francis said, "Of what value is it to walk to a place to preach, unless our walk is also our preaching."

Regarding the Seven Sacraments and the doctrine of Salvation, it is hard to say how much Francis understood about the Gospel. Although he never expounded the Gospel clearly in his writings, his lifestyle was in clear contrast to the papacy and the heresies of the Roman Catholic Church. I would say that he perhaps did more to expose the corruption and the vanity of much of the Catholic clergy by his righteous living. One could say that the deepest desire of Francis' life was to be like Christ – to think, act, and walk like Him.

You can appreciate how Francis teaches us something especially important about Jesus: The purpose of His coming was not so that we could simply pray some words to get saved and then merrily carry on in our vain manner of living. Jesus wants to transform our minds. He wants us to live for the next life, leaving behind this life and its pleasures to find satisfaction and purpose in Him. He said, "If anyone comes to me and does not hate his own father and mother and wife and children and brothers and sisters, yes, and even his own life, he cannot be my disciple. Whoever does not bear his own cross and come after me cannot be my disciple" (*Luke 14:26-27*). We ought to love and imitate Christ so much that our other loves, like the love for family and friends, become entirely secondary to the love we have for Christ.

How did Francis come to take such radical steps to follow Christ? Today the Roman Catholic Church calls him a saint, yet he was clearly in stark opposition to the corruptions of the church of his day. So much so, that it was perhaps only his personal friendship with Pope Innocence III that saved him from the fires of the Holy Inquisition.

Francis was the son of rich parents, a family among the elite in the city of Assisi. He was the favored son of his city, being the center of attention for his charisma and social position. Women pursued him, feasts were held in his honor and later he admitted that lust and pride consumed him during those years.

When the city of Assisi went to war, he came down sick and it bothered him immensely to be left behind. When nearly all his regiment was slain in the subsequent battle, he suddenly realized that God had kept Him and that He had a plan for him. From then on, he became a very pensive young man and spent hours alone meditating on the direction of his life.

One day his father sent him to another town to sell merchandise. On the road he saw a leper covered with terrible, contagious sores beside the path, hiding himself in shame. At that moment Francis said that he felt something which he had never felt before – he was overcome with compassion for that leper and longed to help him. He got down from his horse, went toward the man and embraced him with affection, leaving the poor vagabond speechless.

On another occasion, his father again sent him to another town to sell merchandise. On the way home, young Francis saw a church in disrepair and his heart moved him to give a good sum of money to have it rebuilt. His father was furious since it was his money and so Francis fled to that same church in search of refuge. While his father promised to kill him for his treachery, only the church could legally offer the youth protection. The priest there wisely told Francis that it was his obligation to return and be reconciled with his father, humbly asking his forgiveness.

So, in the middle of an important mass in Assisi, with his father seated in a place of honor, Francis surprised everyone by coming into the cathedral and standing before his father. There he declared to his father in front of the whole congregation, "My lord, I happily return not only all the money that belongs to you but even all of my clothing."

He promptly went into the bishop's room, took off his clothes and folded them, placing all the money on top of the clothing and stepped out before the surprised congregation. Here was the son of a rich and powerful man, a charismatic and honorable young man, bowed humbly before his father and completely naked before the eyes of everyone in the cathedral. Then he proclaimed, "I have decided to serve God." Everyone was left in a shocked silence, as he relinquished fame, wealth, and power, turning instead to follow Christ at whatever cost.

Even though Francis died before reaching 45 years of age, he ended up traveling to hundreds of towns preaching the Word of God, helping the poor, and discipling his followers. At the end of it all, he reflected, "If God can use me, he can use anyone." The key is to be willing; to humble oneself before God and let Him exalt us in His time.

> **Everyone was left in a shocked silence, as he relinquished fame, wealth, and power, turning instead to follow Christ at whatever cost.**

Amid a dark world and a Church ever more corrupt and overwhelmed with greed, Francis gave living testimony to the transforming power of Jesus. Christ does not want us to merely fill the pews and preach from the pulpits. He longs for us to go out and be His hands and feet. Of all Francis' famed sayings, I am most touched by the following, after considering the challenging times in which he lived: "Preach the Gospel at all times. If necessary, use words."

WAS PETER THE FIRST POPE?

In the Vatican, the city where the pope resides, there is a famous wall which has a list of the names of all the popes from the Apostle Peter to the present. The emblem of the papacy includes two keys, which symbolize the power which Jesus gave to Peter as the first leader of the Apostolic Church for him to pass on, one to another, so that his successors could defend the faith. What is the only problem with this idea? That there is not one bit of solid evidence in the Bible or in the history of the early Church to defend this so-called Apostolic succession.

The first one to make the move to declare himself the political and religious leader of Christianity was Leo the Great who declared himself to be "speaking on behalf of Peter" at the Council of Chalcedon in 451 A.D. The other members accused him of being arrogant and had him silenced. Therefore, the first pope as we know it, was Gregory the Great, which finally came about in the year 590. He did not wish to assume the title of being, at the same time, head of the Church and of the Roman Empire, yet in times of such anarchy, this humble monk accepted the role, never imagining what it would later become.

In the following centuries, the Curia was formed, led by cardinals that often wielded power even over the pope. Everything was controlled by money, with religious posts being purchased, something we call "simony." When the pope's position came into question after the Battle of Tours in 732, the curate produced the famous "Donation of Constantine" which declared the pope superior to all other earthly powers. What was the problem with this? It was proved to be a falsification, yet with it taking some 300 years for scholars to discover this, the damage had already been done; the disguised wolf had already ravaged the sheep.

It was proved to be a falsification, yet with it taking some 300 years for scholars to discover this, the damage had already been done; the disguised wolf had already ravaged the sheep.

The struggle for the papacy has its dark chapters, in which much money and blood flowed. Perhaps no time was more terrible than the years from 1309 to 1417, when the pope moved to France and then another pope usurped his place in Rome and finally another one in Pisa, Italy. Three popes at once! And which one kept the title? After much warfare and bloodshed, the second one managed to kill the other two, breaking off the supposed succession from Peter. How abominable! What a terrible lack of respect for the only true Pontiff Maximus of the Church, the Lord Jesus Christ.

CHAPTER 5

MARTIN LUTHER,
Part One

There have been more biographies written about a certain German monk than any other person in history. He caused the mighty Roman Catholic Empire to shudder by his pen and humiliated the papacy by his holy zeal. Standing above Alexander the Great, Plato, Galileo Galilei, and so many others, the name of Martin Luther looms large, that great catalyst of the Great Reformation who forever altered the world half a millennium ago.

The impact of Martin Luther has been global – statues of him are found at the entrances to great universities, his sayings have been inscribed in stone, and his theology has marked Christianity as no one else since Augustine. The story of his life is fascinating and essential for an understanding of the history of the Church.

Between the times of Francis of Assisi and Martin Luther, the immorality and heresy of the Roman Catholic Church grew like gangrene, denying the populace access to the Word of God, imposing innumerable traditions, and demanding

Martin Luther

1483-1546 A.D.

exaggerated offerings which became merely a way of taxing the poor to death. In order to defend its empire and guard against anyone daring to contradict their dogmas, the fearsome Holy Inquisition was used to torture and massacre thousands upon thousands, a great number of them being true believers who had been forced to worship God in secret.

It was at the height of these terrible happenings that Martin Luther was born in the town of Eisleben in the year 1483, in eastern Germany. In 1505, when he was a little more than twenty years old, his fascinating journey towards regeneration began on an afternoon overshadowed by threatening clouds. Being a university student, Martin was on his way home when a torrential rain began to fall. He immediately began running through the heavy mud, which was forming on the road, when a tremendous bolt of lightning fell right in front of him, the flash leaving him nearly blind. It is said that the bolt of lightning threw him into the mud in a terrible fright, soon leaving him with the realization that such a discharge ought to have landed on him and killed him. In a panic he sought to escape from what he thought was the terrible wrath of God for his sins and he cried out like a good Catholic, "Saint Anne, save me and I will become a monk!"

His father would not accept his decision to become a monk because he was poor and had invested so much into his bright son's education hoping that he might help him in his old age. To make matters worse, the young Martin wished to join the Augustinian monks, an extremely strict order with little monetary prospects. Martin persisted in his decision and began a life of what he thought to be devotion to God. He had such a constant fear of God, Whom he considered to be high and mighty and perpetually angry, needing to be appeased at all cost. Years later, Luther meditated, "If anyone could have saved his soul by being a good monk, it would have been me. All the brothers of my monastery are witnesses of this truth. If I had stayed there any longer, I would have killed myself with the vigils, prayers, studies and other efforts to attain holiness."

> *He had such a constant fear of God, Whom he considered to be high and mighty and perpetually angry, needing to be appeased at all cost.*

Martin resided nineteen years under the strict rule of the monastery, at first seeing it as a holy abode, yet later feeling it to be a cage which only made the pain in his soul worse. Day and night, he was tormented by the vision of an angry God, so highly exalted and perfect, that it was impossible for mere man to reach him. This daily reality filled him with chronic ailments and mental anguish.

In order to alleviate his pain, Martin went to confession every day, sometimes for 6 hours at a time! On one occasion Martin took so long in the confessional that he drove the priest to exasperation: "Look," exclaimed the exhausted priest, "if you want Christ to forgive you, come with something big to confess – murder, blasphemy, or adultery – instead of these petty sins." Even so, Luther insisted and went over and over the sins of his life, going to great lengths to recount every sin, even the sins of the mind. He argued that, according to the rules of the Catholic tradition, for one to be forgiven of any sin it must be confessed. For something to be confessed, it had to remembered and recognized, otherwise it would be impossible to remove that guilt before God. If a sin were not confessed, it could not be forgiven, and the person would be condemned before a righteous and omniscient God. This was the impasse that constantly burned in Luther's mind. Since he would never be able to remember every one of his sins in order to confess them, God would always be justified in condemning him.

One important gift Luther had was his faith – whatever he believed to be the truth he accepted and took it to the extreme. He held the belief that a single sin would condemn a man to hell and in that he was right. Little by little he came to the realization that the way of perfection is impossible for a human being. His terrible affliction was so great that it ate away at Luther's mind. He felt lost in his sinful body and without any hope besides his own pitiful efforts.

In his impossible quest to overcome sin, this monk tried a variety of things. One thing he practiced was rigorous asceticism – self-inflicted bodily torture – to try and purge the mind of all worldly passions. Few monks practiced this because they were still in love with sin and materialism. Even so, asceticism leads to another sin when one causes himself physical damage since, "your body is a temple of the Holy Spirit within you" (*I Corinthians 6:19a*). The practice of asceticism gave Luther the false security of having passed hours, maybe even days, "without sinning," yet when he expressed this openly his mind would be filled with pride and hypocrisy. It was the Apostle John who warned us of this danger: "If we say we have not sinned, we make him a liar, and his word is not in us" (*I John 1:10*).

In the continued effort to overcome sin, Martin used to practice a dangerous form of asceticism year-round. He even did it during the German winter, famous for its extreme cold and violent winds. Martin would close and lock his door and then open the window so that the cold air with wind and snow could enter. Then he would take his clothes off and kneel on the floor in prayer, lashing himself with whips that included metal fragments or sharp pieces of bone. He would continue in his prayers even as the blood flowed from his back onto the freezing floor. When the other monks could no longer hear his cries of agony they would go knock on his door and he would respond with painful whispers. After two or three days like that Martin would no longer answer and so the other monks would force the door open and find him splayed out on the floor, starving, covered with blood, blue from the terrible cold, and sometimes unconscious. They would then help their fellow monk recover his strength, heal his wounds and get nourishment. Now, once he felt better, Luther would once again go into his room, close the door, open the window and begin to whip himself. Such was his miserable life as a monk.

We see the gruesome effects of legalism in the life of Luther, because "The law was our guardian until Christ came" (*Galatians 3:24a*). The first step in understanding the infinite worth of Christ and His grace is to understand the seriousness and darkness of our sin. Until we understand that every thought, attitude, and deed which is not fully in line with God's perfection is sin, we will never appreciate the greatness of Christ's sacrifice for all sinners. If sin is a debt to be paid, then it is an infinite debt, and that requires a payment of infinite value. Where is such a thing to be found? "Behold, the Lamb of God, who takes away the sin of the world!" (*John 1:29b*).

After years of this darkness in his soul, God showed him the remedy. The Father Superior of his monastery felt sorry for Martin Luther and he offered him an opportunity, inviting him to go to a theological college to learn the Word of God. The Father admitted that, if the traditions and rites of the monastery could not give peace to his soul, only the Word could. He had never said a truer word, just like Peter's desperate response: "Lord, to whom shall we go? You have the words of eternal life" (*John 6:68*).

The awful truth is that Luther would become the one in a thousand who was legally eligible to read the Word. And the only Bible that a monk could read was the *Vulgate*, an antiquated Latin translation which very few could understand, and which was not accessible to the masses. The medicine which could heal multitudes was locked away in the profound trappings of a false church which trusted more in irrational traditions and pronouncements of its pope rather that in the eternal Word of God.

Luther tried to understand the Word of God, but the *Vulgate* was exceedingly difficult to understand, and he was not able to learn much from it. It was in 1516 that Desiderius Erasmus published the *New Testament* in a modern form of Latin, along with a copy in Greek in order to defend himself

> **Without knowing it, Erasmus had turned loose a most dangerous weapon which could break down the bulwark of the Roman Catholic Church.**

from the critiques which would surely follow. Few paid any attention to the Greek, yet whoever really wanted to read the unadulterated Word of God in the original language began to learn Greek and to read the sacred text, "As a deer pants for flowing streams, so pants my soul for you, O God" (*Psalm*

42:1). Without knowing it, Erasmus had turned loose a most dangerous weapon which could break down the bulwark of the Roman Catholic Church.

Martin devoured this translation like a starving animal, studying it verse by verse to understand what was taught there. He soon came to understand that the Word does not support many of the traditions which the Roman Catholic Church taught. Where does it teach the perpetual virginity of Mary? The Bible teaches that this blessed woman had sons and daughters with Joseph after giving birth to Jesus (*Matthew 13:55*). What text defends praying for the dead and the doctrine of purgatory? The Word tells of only two final destinies: Hell is overflowing with multitudes who reject God's offer, and the delights of heaven with those who entered through the narrow gate and the rough road which Jesus opened by means of His cross (*Matthew 7:13-14*). Where does the Word teach us to endlessly repeat ancient, memorized prayers? Jesus said, "When you are praying, do not use meaningless repetition as the Gentiles do, for they suppose that they will be heard for their many words" (Matthew 6:7, *NASB*).

In his desperation to find the true religion of Jesus Christ, Luther traveled to Rome – the cradle of the Roman Catholic Church. It was there that the spiritual bankruptcy of the people and hypocrisy of those who should be teaching them the Word awoke an impassioned, holy zeal in the heart of this German monk. The grace which Jesus once offered freely to everyone now had a price-tag on it and it was only for those who followed the traditions of the papacy. He discovered that the entrances to cathedrals were markets which offered "hairs of the Apostles," "paving stones Jesus had walked on," and "slivers of the cross of Christ." Innumerable crowds lined up to visit the remains of John the Baptist to kiss his bones and afterwards go on toward the Basilica of Saint Peter. During the day, the cardinals warned the poor against immorality and every kind of excess, yet at night they themselves were drunk with liquor and lying among silk sheets with prostitutes.

Martin Luther returned from Rome as a child bereft of his mother, because his last hope had been the restoration and reformation of the Church. Little by little this vision faded away and he found himself facing a terrible decision – should he fight against hope to transform the Roman Catholic Church or keep silent? Luther knew very well what he ought to choose, and it filled him with trepidation. It would mean excommunication followed by persecution and certain death under the Holy Inquisition. Even so, the Lord illuminated and inspired him with supernatural courage. "So everyone who acknowledges me before men, I also will acknowledge before my Father who is in heaven, but whoever denies me before men, I also will deny before my Father who is in heaven" (*Matthew 10:32-3*).

On the 31st of October 1517, Dr. Martin Luther made public his famous *Ninety-five Theses*, using the Word of God to challenge some of the most essential traditions of the Roman Catholic Church. That day the Great Reformation was ignited, an event which would transform the world forever. Its impact would be so overpowering and world-wide that it would shake up the Curia itself. He could not hold back any

That day the Great Reformation was ignited, an event which would transform the world forever.

longer since he knew the truth of the Gospel and what the people needed – the Word of God. But would he be able to escape the ceaseless and frightful threat of the Pope and the Holy Inquisition?

SOME TRIVIA ABOUT MARTIN LUTHER BEFORE THE REFORMATION:

- When Martin was an adolescent, Christopher Columbus discovered the Americas. He was also a contemporary of Michelangelo who was painting the Sistine Chapel when Luther was teaching theology in Wittenberg.

- His last name was actually "Luder," but since it didn't sound as sophisticated, coming from a poor family, he later changed it to Luther.

- Luther's favorite subject in school was music, but he had to leave it behind when he entered the monastery.

- The first time he ever saw a Bible was when he was 20 years old, since so few people were authorized to read it.

CHAPTER 6

MARTIN LUTHER,
Part Two

To believe in coincidences is nearly as absurd as believing that the sun only shines when you need it or that the birds only sing when there is someone to hear them. God is sovereign and He already knows perfectly well all that has happened, will happen, and even all the hypothetical possibilities in between. In no way does this negate man's free will, but it does give us peace to know that everything has a purpose. The will of God is followed when we seek to do it, even though we know that everything that has happened was already known by God before the creation of the universe. The key is found in God's invitation to each person to long to know, obey, and follow our Creator.

The Bible is full of stories of men and women of God who chose to obey, even when it meant loss, danger, or hardship for themselves. In what we call coincidence or hardship, God presents us an opportunity to prove our faith. Mary, a young woman from Nazareth, suddenly heard the Lord's impossible command and she responded, "Behold, I am the servant of the Lord; let it be to me according to your word" (*Luke 1:38*), even though she knew that getting pregnant before marriage would be repudiated by her people. The Apostle Peter, whom the Jewish leaders threatened and jailed, responded in the same way by preferring to preach the truth by declaring before the council: "Which is right in God's eyes: to listen to you, or to him?" (Acts 4:19, *NIV*) Moses before Pharaoh, David in front of Goliath, and Daniel's friends in the presence of Nebuchadnezzar are even more examples of this wonderful internal strength that is received by those who seek to obey God, come what may.

What is it worth to say we love the Lord if we are not ready to obey him? When we find ourselves in situations that test the love which we profess for God, is that mere coincidence?

> *Martin Luther is merely one in a long list of Christ's followers who risk their lives out of love for God.*

Coincidences simply do not exist, and as rare and improbable as circumstances might appear, so much more ought we to recognize the Hand of a wise Creator. It should be of no surprise that the Lord wants to prove our faith, for as He did with our forefathers, even so He does with us today. Martin Luther is merely one in a long list of Christ's followers who risk their lives out of love for God.

As we saw in the previous chapter, Luther had returned from Rome disillusioned and facing a dangerous dilemma – to try to transform the Roman Catholic Church or to say nothing. The Roman Catholic Church needed to make radical and deep changes in order to take out all the filth and corruption which made it so abominable in the Lord's sight. Everyone knew this, even its priests and monks, and not only those secret groups who were being persecuted by the Holy Inquisition. It is one thing to see the problem and quite another to face it and try to make a change. Many believers and church leaders know very well the problem which infects their lives or their churches, but they are not ready to make painful changes. It is easier to just point the finger and wait for someone else to be the courageous one. I suppose that Luther never dreamed he would be igniting a scandal which would be the catalyst of such profound transformation on the day he decided to so ferociously attack the corruption within the Roman Catholic Church. Even so, it was no accident. Looking back, Luther recognized that the supposed coincidence which occurred the 31st of October 1517, was really the Hand of God putting his faith to the test.

The supposed coincidence and the seed of what would become known as the Great Reformation began in the following way. Luther, now a Doctor of Theology, was living in Wittenberg, teaching in the university there and preaching the Bible in the congregation. Little by little he was instructing his listeners regarding salvation based on the true Word of God and about the precious Gospel which liberates the soul.

One day a monk by the name Johann Tetzel showed up in those lands, being a preacher of indulgences sent by Rome. This man would set up a whole show in the central plaza using special effects and dramatization to scare people with the fear of death. He would speak especially about purgatory, the place where the Roman Catholic Church says most of the deceased go. The "worst" sinners, being in the minority, went straight to hell and the "best" people were canonized as saints. Since the majority supposedly would go and "purge" their sins in purgatory by suffering an excruciating experience which was said to last thousands of years, this monk would offer an alternative: In place of suffering in purgatory, one could buy their escape from it by acquiring a document called an "indulgence" which would be signed by the Pope himself.

When Johann Tetzel arrived near to the city of Wittenberg, Luther went into a rage and decided to challenge him to a public debate. This led to him writing the famed *Ninety-five Theses* which he nailed to the door of the main church so that everyone might witness his effort. Martin Luther, a simple monk from the north of Germany did not think this would attract too much interest, because it was the custom for dealing with differences in those times. Therefore, he went to bed that night and slept soundly supposing that Tetzel might simply ignore his challenge. What he did not know was that a friend of his took this document and had hundreds of copies printed on the recent invention known as a printing press. These copies flew to every corner of the continent. Within only a few days, all of Germany was reading this document and before the end of the month it had made it to the Vatican.

In this document Luther published ninety-five reasons why the practice of indulgences was anti-Biblical. He also questioned the idea of purgatory among other corrupt practices of the Catholic Church. At the time, he thought that the papacy itself would agree with his conclusions since he had based every argument on the Word of God. Yet his document was interpreted as a frontal attack on the Roman Catholic Church and lit the fuse of such a frightening revolution that the pope himself had to take drastic steps to try to quench it. The Roman Catholic Church quickly warned Luther that they could excommunicate him, which would expel him from the Catholic Church. In that day and age, this was feared above everything else. It was then that he saw how God was opening a great opportunity to give the world what it needed so badly – the truth.

And, what caused Luther to write such a powerful document? Johann Tetzel was teaching that a person could buy his entrance straight into heaven: "As soon as a coin in the coffer rings, a soul from purgatory springs," he used to chant from town to town. As we said before, he used fear tactics and taught things that were not in the Bible, and in this way thousands upon thousands were crushed down further into poverty by purchasing indulgences for their dead relatives. Johann was not the only one doing this; it was being practiced all over Europe and was sanctioned by the pope himself who had commissioned priests to this work. This horrible act inflamed Luther so much because he knew well enough that the money from these indulgences went straight to Rome to continue constructing the Basilica of Saint Peter. How could they justify the Germans suffering hunger while this church built an opulent structure so that the wealthy could continue playing at religion? Luther attacked the practice of indulgences by stating: "Why doesn't the pope build the basilica with his own money? He is richer than King Croesus. It would be better for him to sell the Basilica of Saint Peter and give the money to poor citizens who are being shamelessly robbed by the sellers of indulgences."

Besides this, Luther squarely opposed the concept that any man could forgive sins, since that is nothing less than blasphemy against the authority which is God's alone. Referring to this subject, Luther said, "I declare that the pope has no jurisdiction over purgatory… If the pope has power to deliver from purgatory whoever he wants, why in the name of love doesn't he abolish the need for purgatory by letting them all go free?" With this argument he disarmed all the defense of human authority to forgive sins while also proving that indulgences were nothing more than a human invention to raise money. He followed up with sarcasm: "Or did Jesus say, 'if you have a cloak, sell it and buy yourself an indulgence'?"

Luther eventually understood that the Roman Catholic Church was rotten to the core and thus he began to write, research, and even to preach against it, always using the Word of God as his basis. Little by little a group of people came together in Germany and then across all of Europe that desired to abandon the papacy and return to the original New Testament Church which Christ instituted. In Germany, the Lutheran Church appeared, in England the Anglican Church, not to mention numerous autonomous groups which appeared in so many other places. Although they took different names and had different secondary doctrines, they raised up the standard of the Bible and rejected the Roman Catholic Church in an attempt to return to the pure, Apostolic model in the Word of God – some with more success than others. Soon, across Europe the word "reform" echoed, and that worried and angered the Roman Catholic leadership.

In 1521, Luther was called to a council mandated by the pope for the purpose of intimidating him and, if possible, shutting him up forever. By then, Luther had written many books and had a growing desire to translate the Bible into

German. Some inquisitors and prominent theologians were sent to the German town of Worms for this council and given permission to use all resources to neutralize him. They had planned to arrest, torture, and finally kill him, heaping dishonor on him in some *auto da fé* as a dire warning to the people.

In the council, the simple monk honored Jesus Christ in the way in which he stood firm in the face of such cruelty and abuse of power. When they asked him to retract what he had taught and written, he declared before all, including King Charles I, the most important monarch of all Europe: "You must convince me by means of the Scriptures and by reasonable arguments – I cannot accept the authority of popes and councils since these contradict each other – my conscience is entirely captive to the Word of God. I do not have the authority nor the desire to retract what I have written, because that would violate my conscience and that is neither right nor safe to do." It is said that everyone in the auditorium was hushed into absolute silence while Luther sighed and raised his eyes to heaven: "So help me God! Amen."

The populace came together in support of Luther: They sang his name in the plazas and in all the streets even as the council continued. They would not so easily sacrifice their hero, their champion, he who had brought them the true Gospel and sought to deliver them from the tyranny of the Roman Catholic Empire. The monk's enemies soon saw that they had no other option but to set him free. It was at this point that Luther's ministry really began, although painstaking and not without errors. He translated the Bible into German, he wrote many theological tracts and hymns, he married a woman who changed his life for good, and he founded a new movement – the Lutheran Church.

They would not so easily sacrifice their hero, their champion, he who had brought them the true Gospel and sought to deliver them from the tyranny of the Roman Catholic Empire.

It would be unjust to history and to the Lord not to mention some of the faults of this reformer. Luther was a great man worthy of honor, but we must also recognize that he at times spewed hatred against his perceived enemies, the Jewish people, Muslims, and even evangelical movements that were different from his, something which was sadly quite common in those times. He also refused to separate church from state among other harmful things. Even so, Martin Luther, that tenacious German monk, is a testimony of how God can use us if we are willing, because God does not call great men and women – He makes great men and women. Martin was just a man; his strength came from his love of the Scriptures and the power of the Holy Spirit in his life.

And you, are you willing to do great things for God? Are you willing to decrease and let God's will take control?

SOME TRIVIA ABOUT MARTIN LUTHER DURING THE REFORMATION

- It is said that there are more biographies written about Luther than any other person of history, and these focused mainly on his part in the Reformation and the Protestant movement.

- He received a doctorate in Theology and became the head of 10 Augustinian monasteries in Germany until he was officially excommunicated in 1521.

- Luther wrote some 60,000 pages in his lifetime, but he was willing that "all of my books disappear if only the Sacred Scriptures would be made available to read."

- The translation of the Bible into German done by Luther was perhaps the most important work he ever did, giving definition and form to German literature and its language. William Tyndale had a similar impact in England with the translation which he made into English.

The translation of the Bible into German done by Luther was perhaps the most important work he ever did, giving definition and form to German literature and its language.

CHAPTER 7

WILLIAM TYNDALE

It has been said that "without Tyndale, we would have no Shakespeare." Anyone who knows even the slightest thing about literature would agree that William Shakespeare is perhaps the most renowned writer of the Middle Ages, a master of the English language and an inspiration for countless generations of poets and authors. Yet who is William Tyndale? And why is such an exceptional honor afforded him?

The Reformation focuses on the names of Martin Luther, Ulrich Zwingli, and John Calvin in their struggle against the Roman Catholic leadership. It could be argued that Tyndale did more than all of them combined; not because he did as many things as they, but rather that he did one thing with such excellence that he transformed human history once and for all. This man of God is not named in many of the books on Church History and some simply give him a few lines or

> *It could be argued that Tyndale did more than all of them combined; not because he did as many things as they, but rather that he did one thing with such excellence that he transformed human history once and for all.*

William Tyndale

1495-1536 A.D.

mere mention. The truth is that the Church needed people like Tyndale, those silent warriors who worked to glorify God without any need for human recognition. In Tyndale, the English intellectual, we learn a crucial lesson – it is better to do one thing with excellence than ten with mediocrity.

William Tyndale (1495-1536) was born and raised in Gloucestershire, England, an important port in the southeast of the country. Little is known about his childhood or youth, although it is probable that he may have been influenced by the Lollards, a pre-Reformation group that secretly rejected the Roman Catholic Church. Their founder, John Wycliffe (1330-1384), was a great intellectual and theologian who publicly attacked the papacy and the false doctrines of the Roman Catholic Church. He survived, thanks to the distance of England from the Vatican and due to his position as professor in the prestigious university of Oxford. This theologian translated the Bible from Latin to English, and even though it was a coarse and incomplete work, it is something that Tyndale must have read in his youth.

It was illegal to possess a Bible in the common tongue of England, just like in the rest of Europe; having the Word of God in the language of the people was a crime punishable by death. Only the priests could read the Holy Scriptures and the only permissible interpretation was the one given by the "doctors" of the Roman Catholic Church. Tyndale knew well the impact which Wycliffe's translation had had upon the English masses, and little by little a fire began to burn within him, an earnest desire to help his people. In Europe, the Protestant movement was bursting forth, something that began as a murmur had grown into a deafening roar, and the source of their energy was the Bible. Tyndale knew that the key to liberate his people from the tyranny of the pope, the evil political leaders, and the corrupt priests was to translate the Bible into English. But for him to produce the first Bible in English translated from the original languages and make it available to the masses would cost an enormous amount of effort and sacrifice.

To accomplish such a project, first he needed adequate preparation. Tyndale was always a reserved man and not much has been documented about his life, and that is why the first historical detail about him is his graduation from the Magdalen University. He probably had studied first in Oxford where the influence and the writings of two important men would mark him for life – John Wycliffe, already dead by then, and Desiderius Erasmus. It is said that Tyndale was a brilliant student, a real prodigy, being able to earn multiple doctorates.

Desiderius Erasmus was a Catholic theologian who lived in the same era as Luther and Tyndale, and in many ways, he agreed with what they taught. He was opposed to the corruptions of the Roman Catholic Church, yet he expressed it in whispers and disguised it with irony and sarcasm, because he feared the horror of excommunication. Who can blame him? The pressure to remain quiet was strong, especially for a man of such talent and reputation, whose salary came from the Vatican itself. It is too bad that he never left the Roman Catholic Church, but even so, he managed to influence and support the Reformation in a massive way. He clearly knew that the masses deserved to have the Bible which in turn would deliver them from the corruptions of the Roman Catholic Church:

I absolutely repudiate people who desire that the Holy Scriptures not be translated and read by the masses. For, do you think Christ taught such a complicated doctrine that only a few theologians can understand it? Do you think that the strength of the Christian religion rests upon the ignorance of the people? ... Jesus wanted his mysteries to be disseminated as widely as possible. I would prefer that every woman, even those in the lowest strata of life, might read the Gospels and the Epistles of Paul; I desire that those writings be translated into every language of the human race so that they could be read and studied by all.

For anyone else, such words would mean immediate excommunication, but since he was so brilliant and valuable to the Roman Catholic leadership, they left him alone. I wonder what would have happened if Erasmus, this great intellectual and lover of the Word of God, had openly joined the Reformation. The difference between Erasmus and Tyndale is that one merely saw the problem while the other attempted to do something about it. One died between silk sheets with wealth and recognition, while the other was burned alive for defending his faith. Jesus is not content with us knowing the truth, for we must put it into practice.

In spite of this, Erasmus did leave his mark on the Reformation, giving them what they so desperately needed – a complete copy of the *New Testament* in Greek, taken from the libraries of the Vatican itself and published for the whole world. The best efforts of Martin Luther and William Tyndale were greatly helped by the work of Erasmus, since both would translate the Bible from the original into their native tongues.

One day Tyndale, after many years of study and keeping his sympathy for the Protestant movement a secret, clearly saw God's purpose for his life. It was in 1522, while working as the tutor for the children of a rich family, that a priest came to the house for dinner. The conversation eventually turned to the theme of the importance of the Scriptures and these two got into a heated discussion. Suddenly the priest said something truly sacrilegious: "We would be better off without the Word of God to be left only with the pope's words." Doctor Tyndale was filled with holy zeal and when he heard those blasphemous words he exploded, "I repudiate the pope and all his laws! If God gives me but few more years of life, I will cause the plowboy to know more about Scriptures than you do!" While Tyndale did not then pay for his outburst of courage, he was marked as a Protestant and had to take extreme precautions from then on.

This desire to produce a Bible in English and make it accessible to all the people consumed his thoughts and exhausted his resources. A friend of his, seeing how he studied and focused so intently on this work, later said of William, "He was always singing the same note." Tyndale wanted to produce a Bible of excellence, not merely a precise translation, but one that kept the original meter, poetry, and literary beauty. As a theologian, he knew very well the Hebrew and the Greek and could therefore savor the words of the Bible in its original tongue, something he longed to replicate for his countrymen.

> **This desire to produce a Bible in English and make it accessible to all the people consumed his thoughts and exhausted his resources.**

The task was nearly impossible. The work of translation is an artform, and few can communicate the full sense of what is said in another language and another cultural context. How could one replicate the words of Jesus spoken some 1500 years before to Galileans so that the message would still resonate with Englishmen, many of whom could barely even read?

To achieve his task, Tyndale persevered in learning the languages which would help him correctly translate the Word of God. It is said that he learned seven languages "natively," which is an amazing feat. The most important languages for this work were Hebrew, Greek, and English. The last is perhaps surprising since one supposes that anyone would know his own native language well. In fact, this was quite a challenge since it is said that there were then so many varying dialects that a person traveling from one part of England to another could hardly be understood. To understand this, we might liken the differences to what one finds today between Portuguese and Spanish. It is also worth considering that in those days, works written in English were scarce and very few even knew how to read.

William Tyndale basically created a common English language which everyone could understand, written in a simple form which everyone could grasp, while still being able to add the poetry and beauty that is found in the original texts. And what is the most surprising thing? He did it alone, and in a little less than a decade he nearly finished the entire Bible. Nowadays hundreds of theologians, editors, and translators are used in completing a new translation of the Bible. During this time, Tyndale also worked under threat of persecution, a scarcity of good manuscripts, and limited resources. Even so, his heart burned with an unquenchable desire: a love for his people and for the liberty that the Word of God would give them.

As he was finishing his work, Tyndale looked for a publisher which would print it for him, but they were all afraid of the English government and the choleric King Henry VIII. Tyndale also had to put up with Catholic theologians who attacked him fiercely and pined to kill him. The worst of those was the famous theologian Thomas More, who wrote nearly a million words in different publications against William Tyndale, but in his defense, Tyndale did not write more than a few thousand words. Such was the humility of this man, for he knew that his work was for the glory of God even if the world would not recognize it!

Tyndale took his precious translation of the Bible to Europe and in 1526, enduring much difficulty and suffering, finally found a place to print his life's work. Soon the copies infiltrated England by the thousands and shops in every town and city sold them. The English people snatched up the Bibles with great delight, like hungry cubs at the sight of food. The English government, pressured by its alliance with the Roman Catholic Church, was infuriated. Where had these Bibles been produced? How were they coming into the country? Where was Tyndale?

Tyndale's Bibles came into the country hidden in the bales of cotton which were imported in his native town of Gloucestershire. In the intent to block their distribution, the government bought up Tyndale's Bibles, yet that only gave Tyndale more funding to continue printing and flood the market with the precious Word of God.

In the year 1535, Doctor Tyndale was betrayed by a friend in whom he trusted. He was led into a dark alley in Brussels where soldiers arrested him roughly. The soldiers soon felt sorry for him since they saw that he was a simple man, good and humble – just like our Savior. After sixteen months of horrific tortures and imprisonment under the Holy Inquisition, Tyndale was strangled nearly to death and then burned alive before the people for whom he had given all. His last words were not vengeful, instead they were merciful: "Father, open the eyes of the King of England." This was directed at Henry VIII, the wicked English monarch.

Years later, the same King Henry VIII gave up the struggle against the Protestants and decided to join them, mostly for political reasons. Since he had openly repudiated Tyndale's Bible, he ordered a new translation to be done using the best theologians and translators in the land. Later, the process was repeated under other English kings until King James had the famed *King James Bible*, the version which bears his name. Many in those days claimed that it was a miracle when all the different editors, some working separately and in different places, came out with a Bible that was 90% identical. Do you know why? Because 90% of the translation had already been done by Tyndale and all the theologians simply plagiarized his outstanding work.

The Bible would become the soul of the English-speaking world: its educational, political, and religious systems were based on it. By this means, the Gospel reached the whole world. How did the Word of God make its way to the Americas or Asia, for example? You could say, "Thanks to William Tyndale," and you would not be far from the truth.

THE RADICAL REFORMERS, THE FIRST EVANGEL-ICALS

Ten years after Martin Luther published his *Ninety-five Theses* in 1517, Protestant churches sprung up all over Europe. Each country had its own story: in England they separated from Rome because their king wanted to marry another woman against the will of the pope. In Germany it was initially for theological reasons, but then the local government got behind the movement since they were tired of the heavy hand of the Catholic Church. Spain, Italy, and for a time, France remained strongholds of the Roman Catholic Church.

Switzerland was a special case, led by the reformer Ulrich Zwingli and later with the rise of John Calvin, that great theologian of the Reformation. They formed protected city-states, each with its own government where Protestant Christianity was practiced freely right next to the border with Italy. The theology of the Protestant churches was sound, yet some of the traditions they maintained were almost identical with the Catholic ones. The Anglican, Lutheran, and other Protestant churches kept the separation between clergy and laity, they still baptized infants, and they had no notion of separation between church and state.

When a certain group of Christians asked Ulrich Zwingli if he could listen to their ideas to see if they were Biblical or not, he expelled them from the city and absolutely refused to dialogue with them. Even though the initial reformers had done well in rediscovering the Gospel and the power of the Word of God, they needed to be even more transformed by these radical reformers. That is what the Anabaptists were about, the group that Zwingli threw out of his congregation, and against whom Luther was extremely harsh, despite their common enemy being the Roman Catholic Church. The Anabaptists wanted to return to the roots of the Apostolic Church.

Ironically, they followed the famous *regulating principle* that Ulrich Zwingli himself had taught: "If the Bible teaches it, we do it. If the Bible does not teach it, we do not do it."

> **The Anabaptists wanted to return to the roots of the Apostolic Church.**

There was a lot of pride among theologians in that era, even outside of Catholicism, with each one proclaiming their own interpretation as truth. There were tremendous debates between Luther and Zwingli over certain points. Instead of holding a healthy discussion based on the absolute Word, they each insisted on having the last word.

This violent rejection forced the Anabaptists to flee for their lives, living in forests, caves, and places far from civilization. Danger was constant and terrible, but they refused to seek protection from the government, preferring to practice pacifism, just like the early Christians during the Roman persecution had. They also practiced baptism of adults who had converted to Christ and that is why they got their name – Anabaptist means "re-baptized." Their desire was to constantly return to the purity of the Apostolic Church.

Their first leaders included Conrad Grebel, Michael Sattler and Menno Simmons. The modern evangelical movement, which includes Mennonites, Baptists, Reformed, Open Brethren, and many more, comes from them. Little by little the Christian countries understood that these groups were not enemies and began to give them certain freedom of assembly, beginning in the United States.

CHAPTER 8

GEORGE WHITEFIELD AND JOHN WESLEY

Is it possible to have great success in the ministry yet fail at home? Is it right before the Lord to put ministry before one's immediate family?

The Bible clearly shows that God places high esteem on marriage and the family. In fact, He has made it the main building block of society and regards it as a reflection of the unity that is found in the Trinity itself (*Genesis 1:27*; *John 17:21*). Only our relationship with God ought to occupy a more important place in our life than that of our family unit. If we are children, this means parents and siblings take this second place (*Ephesians 6:1*), and if we are married, this means one's spouse and children (*Genesis 2:24*). How many great missionaries, preachers and pastors have paid dearly by forgetting this!

George Whitefield, along with his great friend, John Wesley, are recognized as two of the greatest preachers of all time. These men sparked the most important revival in the history of the United States – the "Great Awakening" (1732-1750), traveling ceaselessly and preaching with great fervor to

George Whitefield

1714-1770 A.D.

thousands upon thousands. They are both worthy of admiration and imitation, with their courage and perseverance for the Lord. That said, both shared a great weakness – they put the ministry before the family, a dangerous and destructive sin. Today this error is repeated almost without any objection in the life of any number of Christian leaders. We would do well to appreciate the good in the life of George and John, but we must be mindful of the dishonor that they brought upon the Lord by neglecting their marriages.

George Whitefield (1714-1770) was born in England and became a great friend of John Wesley (1703-1791) and his brother, Charles. When they were studying together in seminary, John organized the "Holy Group," composed of those three men and some other close friends. John methodically detailed what they should do with their time, minute by minute, taking pains to not fall into sin. Ironically, they all later acknowledged that none of them were saved at the time. Here lies a great warning against legalism, to think that one is saved by things that he does or to claim that one can reach perfection in this life (*I John 1:10*). This dangerous tendency towards perfectionism and legalism which was applied methodically to his lifestyle and which he taught to others kept dogging John Wesley all his life, and thus the Wesleyan movement which bears his name is better known as the Methodist Church.

> **George Whitefield, along with his great friend, John Wesley, are recognized as two of the greatest preachers of all time.**

After some years living in this way, John Wesley traveled to the South of the United States, since he thought that the sin of lust, his great weakness, would be lessened in the New World. It did not turn out that way and there he fell in love with a young lady in a church that he was pastoring. She refused his advances, preferring instead to marry another man. This made John so angry that he excommunicated them both from his congregation! It was at that time that he decided to return to England, discouraged and confused, wondering what the Lord wanted to do with his life.

On his way home, a terrible storm nearly destroyed the ship he was sailing on. John hung on to the ship's ropes with his heart sinking in desperation and fear. Suddenly, near to him, he saw a group of believers singing to the Lord and praying – he could see the peace that they had. His eyes were opened to see that he, although the minister of a church, was not a child of God and so he asked for help from those faithful brothers. Amid such a storm, John found peace for his soul. His favorite hymn, "And Can It Be" gives testimony to this moment:

Long my imprisoned spirit lay,

Fast bound in sin and nature's night;

Thine eye diffused a quick'ning ray—

I woke, the dungeon flamed with light;

My chains fell off, my heart was free,

I rose, went forth, and followed Thee.

When Wesley returned to England, he found another church to pastor, since by profession he was a minister of the

Anglican Church. His love for the Word of God and his passion for the Gospel made for a revolution in his new congregation, although not everyone approved. Pretty soon his new style, so strong and passionate, received harsh criticism on the part of ministers who felt that he was too "radical" and even "exaggerated." They removed him from the pastorate, and he was left without work.

In another part of the English Isle his friend, the minister George Whitefield, had suffered a similar experience, also being repudiated by the Anglican Church. George had begun to preach when he was 22 years old and his passion for preaching the Gospel burned in him like a fire. In his first years, Whitefield was the minister of an Anglican church, the official denomination of England. Soon he was lambasted by older ministers who called him an "actor" and even "crazy," because of how he shouted from the pulpit, often with tears for lost souls, and other times ranting about the consuming fire of God which would come down on those who refused the Gospel.

George Whitefield was never a man to give up nor be quieted when he knew he had the truth. Truth does not depend on the acceptance of multitudes but belongs to God, and when the multitudes shun God, wise men must hold the truth and struggle to make it known. On one occasion, while preaching in London, Whitefield offered this defense of his passionate style:

"Let me tell a story," he began. "The Archbishop of Canterbury in the year 1675 was acquainted with Mr. Butterton the [actor]. One day the Archbishop . . . said to Butterton . . . 'pray inform me, Mr. Butterton, what is the reason you actors on stage can affect your congregations with speaking of things imaginary, as if they were real, while we in church speak of things real, which our congregations only receive as if they were imaginary?' 'Why my Lord,' says Butterton, 'the reason is very plain. We actors on stage speak of things imaginary, as if they were real and you in the pulpit speak of things real as if they were imaginary.'" Having said this Whitefield burst out in a thunderous voice: "Therefore, I will [shout loudly], I will not be a velvet-mouthed preacher."

Proclamations like this made a lot of enemies for George Whitefield. Ministers and preachers who were envious of his fame felt uncomfortable with the threat to their suave and professional style. When they told him that he should change his style of preaching – for he would sometimes jump, vociferate, and wave his arms – Whitefield replied that he was not putting on a show: "If your house were burning down with your son inside, you wouldn't be acting!" Here we learn the cruel truth that sometimes the worst enemies of the Christian who is dedicated to the Lord are found right in our own churches.

Whitefield eventually decided to leave London and at the age of 24 he preached in the open air for the first time, something entirely novel and unacceptable in the eyes of the Anglican Church. From then on and until his death at 55, it is estimated that he preached daily, some 1000 times a year, which would equate to more than 30,000 times in his lifetime! George travelled 14 times to Scotland and 7 times to the United States, something that was exceedingly difficult in those days with sailing ships and horse-drawn carriages. George Whitefield would preach and preach, and after sleeping a little and traveling some more he would preach and preach some more. That was the life this man of God led; he was in love with the Word of God and desperate to share the Good News with everyone. Once he said, "It would be impossible for me to travel with another person for fifteen minutes without talking to him about Jesus."

John Wesley, when he saw all the doors closing for him in the ministry, was invited by George Whitefield to be introduced to open air preaching. Wesley accepted, although he did so with reservations because it was something so radical and innovative. What John saw transformed him forever:

George was standing upon a hill near a dark and dangerous coal mine entrance waiting for the workers to come out. In the afternoon, the miners began to come out of the dark pit, their faces covered with black soot. Whitefield invited them to listen to him and quickly a multitude of them surrounded the hill, eager to hear. George had an extraordinary talent for oratory, with a captivating way of speaking. One might argue that he was the most powerful and important preacher in the history of the Church. A listener one time said that Whitefield had been "born to be a preacher" and another claimed that he "can bring tears to men's eyes simply by the way he pronounces Mesopotamia," although surely stated with some exaggeration.

John observed the moving of the Holy Spirit in the lives of those miners. Suddenly these black faces, covered with soot, began to show small, white rivers forming on their faces, from the tears which came down as they heard of the great love of God for them. John Wesley never forgot that glorious moment where he felt God calling him to also preach in the open air.

> *Suddenly these black faces, covered with soot, began to show small, white rivers forming on their faces, from the tears which came down as they heard of the great love of God for them.*

Whitefield and Wesley would pass the next decades traveling, separately, over the whole United States, England, and Scotland, preaching ceaselessly. It is said the Wesley preached more than 40,000 sermons and traveled over 250,000 miles on horseback (in normal usage, a person might drive his car that far in the space of ten years) and also managed to publish more than 400 books. It is exhausting to even think of such feats!

Along with all their heroic efforts they also had great weaknesses, especially John Wesley. For many contemporaries, Wesley was always second best to Whitefield who was the better preacher, and this caused jealously in his heart. Besides these feelings, Whitefield and he had different points of view regarding free will, with Whitefield being a Calvinist and Wesley an Arminian. While George thought it to be a secondary doctrine, Wesley used it as a special weapon to publicly defame and thus "bring down" Whitefield. He even published a magazine to attack Calvinism and especially his one-time close friend.

It is said that a youth was curious to know what Whitefield thought about all the criticism which Wesley published against him. The young man, wanting to win favor with the preacher, said, "Do you think we shall see Mr. Wesley in heaven?" To which Whitefield replied, "I fear [we will] not," to the surprise of everyone, but then he proceeded to explain himself, "for he will be so near the eternal throne and we at such a distance, we shall hardly get sight of him." Whitefield never criticized his friend publicly, because he understood that the work of the Lord was a team effort, and that competing held no value. If anyone does something well or even better than us: Glory to God! Whitefield's response is a great example of how to return good for evil, even as Jesus taught (*Luke 6:35*).

Whitefield also had a great weakness, one that Wesley also shared – they neglected the role of the family in their pursuit of the ministry, thus dishonoring the Lord. At first, Whitefield did try to marry a woman he had fallen in love with. But this new sensation was a hard one for him to grasp, feeling that love for her was a rival for his love of Jesus. When he proposed marriage to her, he did it in such a way that it did not include any mention of love, instead speaking of the responsibilities of it as though marriage were a necessary evil. Thanks to her prudent father who would not let her be carried away by the fame of the great preacher, she rejected his advances. Whitefield then took an interest in Elizabeth and married her, yet admittedly without feeling any love for her.

Whitefield had promised, "When I am married, I will preach no fewer sermons than I did when I was single." Even during their honeymoon George preached twice a day. At its end, he quickly left on a trip, yet she decided to stay at home since the trip would be long and involved an extended time away. On one occasion, he did not come home for two years and he barely kept in touch with her. She lost four pregnancies and her only son died before he reached his first birthday. All of this she had to bear alone. Whitefield brought his wife great suffering and sadness, even though he was always courteous to her on the rare occasions they spent together. In private, she stated that other people knew her husband far better than she ever did.

Wesley fell into the same error when he married Molly. He spoke often about love and that marriage was the will of God, yet he did not know how to love his wife or care for her (*Ephesians 5:25*). He would travel for months on end and his letters to his wife were merely a list of rules and methods, treating her almost like his slave. When she asked him to come home so they could share life together he rejected it completely: "Be contented to live a private and insignificant life, known and loved only by God and by me."

Molly, being older than he was, tried to support him, but she could not withstand the long journeys and eventually ended up staying at home without him. As the years passed, she became aware of a certain secretive tendency of her husband and she accused him on several occasions of committing adultery and of writing love letters to other women. Molly was growing ever more burdened by jealousy, insecurity, and a feeling of not being loved by John. On two occasions she left him because she was tired of putting up with his insults and manipulation. The second time she did not come back, but not before hearing her husband say, "I hope I never see your horrid face again."

Now, Molly was not the victim either, for she did not know how to treat her husband, fighting and arguing with vehemence instead of seeking reconciliation. Their marriage was clearly not healthy nor good because she didn't respect him, and he didn't love her.

Although the sad story has been recounted in many ways, it is said that when his wife left him for the last time, he did not go in search of her for many years. Finally, repentant, he went to her father's house to seek for her. The old man said that she was in the back and that he could go and see her there. When he could not find her, he returned to his father-in-law. He told him that Molly had died and that it was her tombstone which he could find out back. In the end, John was never reconciled with Molly nor with Whitefield; he was a man who began so well and did so much for the Lord but finished so poorly.

It does not matter how much recognition we get in the ministry, if we fail in the area of family all the good done will be annulled in this hypocrisy. Thank God that he could still use men like John and George despite their serious deficiencies! May it be an example for us about organizing priorities: God first, then family, and then ministry or work.

• •

It does not matter how much recognition we get in the ministry, if we fail in the area of family all the good done will be annulled in this hypocrisy.

• •

THE MISSIONARY MOVEMENT

When we study the history of the Church, there is something which stands out due to its absence. Where are the missionaries? The Apostolic Church was consumed with the burden to share the Gospel, with many believers following the steps of the Apostles and dying for their faith. Yet when the Emperor Constantine established Christianity as the official religion of the Roman Empire, everything changed, and the great commission was nearly forgotten. Suddenly the focus switched to battling heresy as we have seen in Athanasius and Augustine. Later, the empire fell, and Europe found itself immersed in the Dark Ages; the struggle at that time was one of survival. Charlemagne brought peace and stability to Europe in the 700's but little by little the leaders of the Church began to have less regard for the Word of God. The ages prior to the Reformation were full of corruption. Under the new world power, the Roman Catholic Church, the true believers had to flee for their lives, persecuted by the last Crusades and the dreaded Holy Inquisition. The believers of various groups, like the Waldenses, for example, used to share their faith, although always in secret. The Reformation brought many liberties to a growing number of countries, but Christianity took a long time to realize the need for missions.

At times, they lacked the resources or the liberties to do it, and besides that, they did not know how enormous the world was. And what happened with the thousands of thousands during so many centuries who died without hearing the name of Jesus? I believe we need to trust in God, even as Abraham did: "Shall not the Judge of all the earth do what is just?" (*Genesis 18:25b*). When the world does not hear the Gospel, we are at fault. Before pointing the finger at those who lived in those distant and dangerous ages, we ought to judge ourselves. What are we doing to raise up the name of the Lord? Why don't we go? And if I can't, how can I help, encourage or team up with those who do go?

The Age of Modern Missions finally began with William Carey (1761-1834). Churches were increasingly full of petty, internal discussions and arguments and William begged the leaders of his church to begin to take an interest in taking the Gospel to the world. They lived in England, a country whose naval strength knew no rival, and for that reason the English people were without excuse. William argued that, if they were getting products from places like India, why shouldn't the English be sharing the greatest Good that there is with them? They did not listen to him. Why? Because he was merely a shoe cobbler, a "Mr. Nobody." But William was so persistent that finally they told him that he ought to stop pestering them with his arguments and supplications and proceed to go himself. William Carey then crossed the seas in an English ship, without financial support, yet with great faith. What he did in India and the stories that were repeated once and again about the work of the Lord there soon moved the church in England and in Europe to action. The revolution that this man began soon caused thousands and thousands of young men to cross the world's frontiers to share the gospel. The cobbler, that "Mr. Nobody," William Carey, today is known as "The Father of Modern Missions." This is the way God works! To Him alone be the glory!

God does not seek great men and women; He makes great men and women. And you…are you willing to be used by God?

CHAPTER 9

GEORGE MULLER

"Let us pray," said George Muller, standing in front of hundreds of children that filled the dining hall. They had the plates, glasses and silverware set out, but there was not a crumb in the house. "Lord," Muller prayed, "we give thanks for the food that we are going to eat. In the name of the Lord Jesus Christ," but before he could say "Amen," someone knocked loudly on the door. The children sat in expectant silence while Mr. Muller went to answer. Standing outside was a man that he had never seen before. The man said he was a baker and he explained that, as he came into town to sell his goods, the wheel of his cart had fallen off right outside Muller's orphanage. A few minutes later, Muller came in with an enormous smile on his face, his arms overflowing with loaves, cakes and pastries.

There is a terrible lie that the devil always uses against us. In his deceitfulness he tries to make us think that our happiness depends on money or praise from others. One of the most joyful men in the history of the Church was George Muller, a man who, although he had little and had suffered much, abounded in good cheer and a great faith. George is

George Muller

1805-1898 A.D.

one on my favorite people of all time, one who inspires me to always do more for the Lord and not to waste time on vain, temporal things.

Muller rightly said: "A servant of God has but one Master. It ill becomes the servant to seek to be rich, and great, and honored in that world where his Lord was poor, and mean, and despised." When asked to give his testimony, he explained, "There was a day when I died; died to self, my opinions, preferences, tastes and will; died to the world, its approval or censure; died to the approval or blame even of my [family] or friends; and since then I have studied only to show myself approved unto God." How did he come to have such a radical conviction?

> *George is one on my favorite people of all time, one who inspires me to always do more for the Lord and not to waste time on vain, temporal things.*

George Muller (1805-1898) was born into a wealthy family in Germany. As a youth he used to steal, first from his father, then from his friends, until he was eventually arrested as a thief. As for education, he eventually decided to study Theology. George admitted that he was not saved then, and that he wasn't the least bit interested in the Word or the ministry. He simply chose that profession because he believed it be the fastest way to make easy money as a minister in the Lutheran Church. What a shame!

When Muller was not studying, he spent his time getting drunk at the bar with fellow students and later, figuring ways to get out of debt. That was when a friend of his, who had given his life to Christ, invited him to a Bible study. The idea wasn't attractive to him, but he pretended to be interested in order to please his friend.

Upon arrival at the Bible study, he was surprised to find it in a house and not in some cathedral. They sang some hymns and then the Word of God was expounded clearly. Muller was shocked. Later, he admitted that nothing in his life had given him such pleasure as that experience. Soon he was coming back daily to the meetings and before the week was out, he was kneeling to pray beside his bed, asking God for forgiveness and asking Him to turn him into a true Christian.

It was a total, transformative change which left his companions perplexed. He no longer went to parties with them, he didn't get drunk, and he wasn't asking for them to loan him money anymore. In place of that, he was spending hours studying the Word of God, focusing on his courses of study, and working honestly to pay for his needs. And this was only the beginning. Six weeks after his conversion, God put a new desire in his heart – to become a missionary. From that day on he had a growing sense of urgency to not waste his life, as he later expressed it: "The longer I live, the more I am enabled to realize that I have but one life to live on earth, and that this one life is but a brief life, for sowing, in comparison with eternity, for reaping."

During this brief, important, and moving period of his life, George had fallen in love with Ermegarde, a beautiful and wealthy young lady who had attended those Bible studies for years. They had plans to be married within six weeks. He supposed that she would also be willing to leave all in order to serve the Lord, like the Word teaches. That is why, after a Saturday meeting, the two of them were sitting together and

Muller told her with deep emotion of his intention to become a missionary along with her. She burst out, "George! What would make you think something so ridiculous? I would never be the wife of a missionary!" Even with an injured heart Muller tried to convince her, yet it was in vain as she responded even more energetically, "Missionaries are poor. They wear ugly clothes, and I would rather be dead than ride in their horrible carriages. Forgive me, George Muller, but you need to decide between missions and me… Become a lawyer or a doctor and leave that business of being a missionary to other people who don't have anything better to do with their lives!"

George went home devastated because he loved Ermegarde and wanted to marry her. He eventually had to break off the relationship and put his faith in God to bring along someone who wanted to serve the Lord in something as honorable as missions. She was mistaken and blinded by materialism, because serving the Lord is the most sublime thing that one could possibly do, even as Charles Spurgeon once said: "If God has called you to be His servant, why stoop to be a King?"

Eventually, Muller moved to England with the intention of preparing himself to become a missionary to the Jews in Europe, but God kept fashioning this plan until he finally saw that his call to missions was right there in England. It was there that he fell in love with Mary Groves, a great woman of God who soon became his wife. They shared so much in common: love for missions and love for the Word of God. It was somewhat strange that he should fall in love with her because she was 33 years old and he was only 25, besides he later admitted that he did not find her very attractive physically, with the "biggest nose he has seen in his life!" Yet she won him by her inner beauty and her willingness to submit entirely to the Lord and to him.

Muller's worst fear regarding marriage was of finding himself enslaved to pleasing his wife and leaving to one side the things of the Lord, like he had seen happen in so many cases. It was she who convinced him, assuring him that they were going to be able do more for the Lord together than single because they shared the same desire. They were married only five months after meeting, he already being the congregational leader with little resources of a meeting place for the new and radical movement known as the Brethren (later called "Open Brethren").

During one of their first nights, this fear was put to the test. Mary was from a wealthy family and had brought with her many things of real value with which she had decorated their little apartment. George came into the house tired and he sat down, looking intently at the way his wife had decorated the house. "They have to go," he said suddenly. She was surprised and asked what he was talking about. He pointed at the decorations and the fancy china, responding, "All of it." The next day, when he came home in the evening, she had sold all the unnecessary articles and given the money to her husband. If Muller were right in asking this of his wife, only God knows, but the courage and submission of his wife would not go unrecompensed.

A week later, Muller surprised his wife again. He had decided he would not charge any salary from the church as was normal for pastors to do; instead, he would accept as from the Lord whatever the believers might give freely. He would not ask for money from anyone ever again! Muller fulfilled his word, and it became something which he practiced his whole life, and even so God never left him in poverty. They went through great needs on innumerable occasions, but in wonderful ways God provided for them. When they had money left over, they took it upon themselves to give it to others who had needs. Mary didn't answer back, but rather she supported the radical thinking of her husband. Muller, referring to the suffering that they went through, explained: "The only way to learn strong faith is to endure great trials."

George Muller is known above all for his faith, and with good reason. The radical thinking which they practiced in the home would also be applied to the ministry. We often wonder what the will of God is, perhaps expecting him to whisper in our ear or send us a message from heaven. Muller taught that the will of God is simply responding to the needs that come our way, be they small or large. Some see the need for doing discipleship, others evangelism, others teaching the Word, others practicing hospitality, etc. To simply respond to the need you see is what it means to do the will of God.

In England at that time there was a terrible problem – an unending number of kids living in the streets. The economy wasn't great and when parents couldn't feed their children, they took them to the poor side of the city and left them to be raised by other children. The factories took advantage of this situation making them work up to 16 hours a day, 7 days a week. Their pay? A miserable plate of food. A great many children were thus raised without parents, without

> **Muller taught that the will of God is simply responding to the needs that come our way, be they small or large.**

hope, without love, and with terrible habits like stealing and lying.

George Muller decided to do something radical, not because he worked with children or because he had a special love for them, but simply because he saw the need and responded. He declared, "God has given me a mission field here, and I will live and die in it." During the greater part of his adult life Muller dedicated himself to giving a home, an education, and love to 10,024 children in 6 enormous homes which they were able to build. Absolutely everything was done through freewill offerings since Muller refused to ask for money or seek promises of support. There were times of great need, like the example given at the beginning of the chapter, but God was faithful to him. This way of operating has become the norm in almost all the ministries and missionary endeavors of the Open Brethren, honoring the conviction of Muller in recognizing the faithfulness of a great God.

Muller not only supported the orphanages, he also preached regularly, being recognized as one of the best expository teachers of the Word in all of England. He was an elder at a large, fervent church; he supported an endless list of ministries, and it was his great delight always to support missions. In all of this, his wife Mary was a truly faithful helpmeet and he loved her dearly. He used to say that when he was with her it was a delight for his soul.

A few years after their marriage, Mary became sick and, within a few days, was on her deathbed. George Muller knelt sadly beside her bed and prayed, "[Lord], if it is good for her and for me, she will be restored again. If not, she won't." Days later, Mary died leaving him a young widower. Can you imagine his pain? What would you feel? Here we see the great character and faith of Muller, because when one goes through great trials, our true self is exposed.

Muller asked to be allowed to preach at the burial of his dear Mary. He held back the tears and spoke tenderly of his beloved wife. The phrase which most impacted the listeners was when he declared, "My heart is at rest. I am satisfied with God." Muller understood that it was the will of God for her to be taken to Heaven; he trusted that God had done everything according to His plan and for George's greater well-being. This great man was so sure of the Lord's care that, even in the worse trial, he found his joy in the Lord. Muller considered that "the first great and primary business to which I ought to attend every day was, to have my soul happy in the Lord." It is told that, above everything else, what people admired most in George was his joy, demonstrated by his wonderful smile and his desire to continually help his neighbor.

Instead of being filled with bitterness or depression, this catastrophic event made his faith grow, leading him to do even more for the Lord. In time, George Muller remarried. His second wife was also a real helpmeet and George loved her deeply.

When he was 70 years old, at a time when many think of retirement or simply enjoying their grandchildren, George Muller launched-out on a new endeavor. Since his youth he had had a great desire to be a missionary, and now he felt he had the liberty to fulfill it. During the next 22 years he dedicated himself to traveling to 42 countries, including parts of Africa and North America. It is said that he preached to more than 3 million people in this time. It is also estimated that by the end of his life he had preached at least 10,000 times. Astonishing!

> Like the old saying goes, "He died with his boots on."

Before his death, Muller commented that he had read the Bible at least 200 times from cover to cover. He prayed daily because it was the desire of his heart to always draw closer to the Lord. And that's the way he was found in the end, at 92 years old, on one of his missionary journeys, kneeling beside his bed – praying. Like the old saying goes, "He died with his boots on."

THERE ARE SO MANY CHURCHES AND DENOMINATIONS, HOW DO I KNOW WHICH ONE IS GOOD?

It has been said that we live today in the new "Era of Heresies," and that you can no longer tell if a church is sound by the name over the door. Some denominations in certain countries have been influenced and turned from their historic stand, and in many cases, you must know the pastor or the leader of the church in order to know if that church is sound. You can't judge a book by its cover, neither can you judge a church by its statement of faith or denominational title. Here are some clues to examine one's church or when looking for a new one:

1. What place is given to the Word of God? God teaches that the power to transform lives is in His Word and in His Holy Spirit. It is essential that the Bible, taught in a way that is unadulterated and in its natural context, be the basis of the church's teaching. No human doctrine or tradition ought to compete with the absolute authority held by Scripture.

2. What Gospel is preached? The Bible focuses on grace – an unmerited gift for everyone who believes in Jesus as the only Savior. We cannot be saved by works, or by keeping the commandments, or by traditions, or by any church or leader, or by money, or by speaking in tongues, or by any spiritual "experience." We are saved by Jesus and this is the Gospel that has been entrusted to us as the greatest gift of the Church. Protect it!

3. Are they always asking for money? One of the most dangerous and notorious tendencies of false teachers is what is called "Prosperity Gospel." In general, this is accompanied by supposed miracles, prophecies, and lots of

sentimentalism, always with the purpose of reaching your pocketbook. Jesus never charged for His miracles or teachings; He did everything out of love for us. The true servant of God trusts in the Lord's provision without having as a priority getting wealthy or famous on this earth.

4. Is there love and unity? Every church has its problems, but where the Spirit of God is, love and reconciliation between brothers ought to be practiced. They should share a fervor for serving the Lord, where each has an important place. There ought to also be freedom from legalism because a legalistic church can squelch your spirit and put out the fire for God.

5. Are they looking beyond their four walls? It has been said that a healthy and growing church is one with missionary vision. This is a secondary requirement, yet I believe that anyone who really loves the Lord wants to be part of what He is doing throughout the world. If, in your church, this focus doesn't exist, perhaps it's time for you to do your part to encourage it.

EPILOGUE

The stories that have been narrated include some of the most important men in the history of the Church, great heroes of the faith. It is common to make the mistake of only seeing their virtues, and on other occasions, when we don't like them much, to only see their faults. But we ought to understand that they were just men, nothing more and nothing less, the same as us. *James* teaches us this about the great, transformative power of God: "Elijah was a man with a nature like ours, and he prayed fervently that it might not rain, and for three years and six months it did not rain on the earth. Then he prayed again, and heaven gave rain, and the earth bore its fruit." (*5:17-8*). It is God who wants and can do great things through us.

There wouldn't be time to tell the great stories of other men and women who transformed the world forever, to the glory and honor of God. What might we say about Peter Waldo? This man was a contemporary of Francis of Assisi. He sold his fortune when he became an evangelist and was later tortured and killed by the Holy Inquisition. What could we say about Gladys Alyward? She was turned down by established missions for her lack of formal Bible training and because she was nothing but a maid in London, yet she persevered in seeking the will of God, eventually receiving honors from the Emperor of China himself for her impact on a national level in that country. Couldn't we also eulogize Eric Liddell? After being a famous rugby player on the Scottish team and winning gold and bronze medals in the Olympic Games in Paris in 1924 and setting a world record, he decided to leave fame and fortune behind to serve as a missionary in China. And can't even more be said about William Carey? He has received the ostentatious title of "The Father of Modern Missions," because he went out as a pioneer to overseas missions even though he began as a humble a shoe repairman.

Heroes! Titans of history! When we look at great people of history it is common to feel small, even useless in comparison. The reason why we study great men and women of history is to be inspired and be encouraged to battle against mediocrity. The more we give over our lives into the hands of God, the more we can see the glorious and transcendental plans which He has for us. Earthly and material things will soon pass, and we would do well to remember the words of C.T. Studd, that great English missionary: "Only one life, 'twill soon be past, only what's done for Christ will last."

We also could become heroes of the faith with acts to resound for all eternity. The essential things for every great man and woman of God in history is a love for the Word of God, a desire to be molded by it and the struggle for excellence. We can also impact those who surround us: our family, our church, our nation or even the whole world. If we decide to put our lives in the hands of God, who knows where that may take us?

REFERENCES USED

1. Augustine of Hippo. *Confessions*.

2. Bainton, Roland H. *Here I Stand*: *A Life of Martin Luther*.

3. Benge, Janet and Geoff. *George Muller: The Guardian of Bristol's Orphans*.

4. Heinze, Thomas F. *Answers to My Jehovah's Witness Friends: Shocking Truths Your Religion Won't Tell You*.

5. McGrath, Alister. *Christianity's Dangerous Idea*: *The Protestant Revolution-A History from the Sixteenth Century to the Twenty-First*.

6. McGrath, Alister. *Heresy: A History of Defending the Truth*.

7. Miller, Basil. *John Wesley*.

8. Murray, Wendy. *A Mended and Broken Heart: The Life and Love of Francis of Assisi*.

9. Shelley, Bruce L. *Church History in Plain Language*. Third Edition.

Made in the USA
Columbia, SC
14 October 2021

47191925R00071